SECRET STRUGGLES

Finding Freedom From Hidden Bondage

Angel Walston

I dedicate this book to my mother, Renee, who I like to call Martha on occasion. Thank you for always supporting, loving, and believing in who God has allowed me to be. I know that I can always depend on you to be my biggest cheerleader.

I love you,

Angel a.k.a. Susie

Contents:

Introduction

Secret Struggles

➤➤〉〉〉〉〉 —————————— 〈〈〈〈〈〈◀

Well, hello there, friend! Oh, you don't know we're friends yet? Ah, well this is awkward. Let me explain...

When you picked up this book, you automatically became friends with me. Whether you wanted to be or not, we're here now, so don't even think about trying to exchange it. Just bring your book close to your heart and let me love you, okay? Cool!

We're going to get real personal all up and throughout this book. I'm talking TMI personal! There'll be some laughs, some tears, and probably some moments where you might not like me very much. That's okay; friendships have their ups and downs. Just know that if I step on your toes with hard-hitting truths, the Holy Spirit stubbed my pinky toe and pulled my card first.

Like any good relationship, friendships require honesty, vulnerability, and accountability. When you think about your closest friends, hopefully they are people who you can have honest conversations with about the real issues you encounter in life. They should be people who don't condemn you but who love you back to Christ and point you in the right direction when you get sidetracked. Sometimes their pointing may feel more like a push or a drag, but it's usually with good intentions; they want what is best for you...And that's where I come in, friend!

Throughout the remaining chapters, we are going to have quite a few honest conversations about real issues that impact our lives, whether we want to acknowledge them or not. We're going to discuss different areas in our hearts that need fixing, and we will address instances in which we need a full-on transplant. I say *we* because I'm in this with you! I'm getting gut-punched with correction and conviction too, so know that you're not alone.

My hope is that as you read through each chapter, you will find a safe place to examine secret struggles in your life. I'll be honest—this likely is not going to *feel* good, but I promise it will work out for your good. How so, you ask? Well, as you start to experience freedom from bondage, past hurts, guilt, and shame, it's likely that dormant issues may rise to the surface. There may be old wounds that you thought you had dealt with already, when in reality, you only covered them instead of allowing them to be healed.

Quite frankly, there will be times that you may not want to deal with your stuff because it will bring up memories and emotions that you aren't ready to handle. It'll be easier to close the chapter than to think about why you do or don't do certain things; keep in mind what is on the other side of you addressing it—your freedom. All I ask is that you have an open heart for the Lord to reveal whatever He desires to reveal to you throughout these pages.

So, what exactly are secret struggles? They are the hidden issues in your life. I say *hidden* because they're usually the areas that you struggle with that no one else knows about. They're the things that you go through in silence as you put on face for church, work, family, friends, and whoever else that you don't want to know what is *really* going on with you. In some instances, your secret struggle may be a sin, such as fornication or coveting, while in others, your struggle may be with fear or depression.

Although the chapters covered are not an exclusive list of all possible secret struggles, I hope that you will be able to use what you learn throughout this book and apply it to those areas that are not listed. One of the things that you will constantly see me talk about that can be applied to any topic not covered, is the importance of identifying the root of the issue. I want to encourage you to take the time to really think about this. It's easy to dismiss actions or behaviors without actually looking at the *whys* behind them. Not on my watch, girlfriend! Don't choose to ignore problems just because yours aren't covered specifically in this book.

The purpose of this book is not to make you feel bad about your issues. Trust me when I say that we all have something that we are struggling with. I have struggled with every single topic covered within this book. Truth be told, I'm currently struggling with a handful of the topics. I'm not here to point out your problems and make myself out to be the one who has it all figured out. That's the furthest from the truth!

My goal is to point you to Christ and to let you know that there's no reason to remain bound when we serve a God who has the power and authority to set us free and make us whole. He desires for us to walk in freedom, yet somewhere along the way, we've allowed life to convince us to settle with being sort-of, kind-of, free.

We'll listen to sermons, attend conferences, and cry during an altar call, but still remain bound. We'll lead, serve, and tell others about Jesus as we continue to be enslaved to bondage. What good is it to find ourselves in church, saved, leading women's groups, and singing on the praise and worship team yet never fully experiencing the freedom that is available through Christ?

I don't know about you, but I refuse to allow bondage to become my norm just because it has been my experience. I won't sit back and allow dysfunction or sin to become comfortable in my life simply because it's what I've grown accustomed to. I won't accept cycles of brokenness or past mistakes to dictate my ability to be free when freedom is readily available to me through Jesus Christ (2 Corinthians 3:17; John 8:36; Romans 8:1-2; Galatians 5:1).

My prayer is that as you identify the secret struggles within your life, you will be able to fully surrender them to God. I am standing in agreement with you for whatever you are believing Him for as you flip through the remaining pages. I declare that chains, strongholds, and generational curses will be broken as you walk in freedom. I'm believing with you that the same power that raised Jesus from the dead will move through your heart to heal, set free, and deliver in Jesus' name.

Chapter 1
Unfulfilled Purpose
Oh Yeah, I Am Supposed to do That

→))))))))——————((((((((←

One of the burning questions we all have at some point in life is, "What is my purpose? What *exactly* am I on this earth for?" Maybe God has already revealed it to you, but you aren't in the season to see it fulfilled yet. Perhaps you're still figuring out exactly what it is and that's perfectly okay, too!

Whether you're walking in purpose now or in the very beginning stages of discovering it, know that we all have a universal purpose in common. When we accept the identity of a believer, we also accept an assignment that sadly a lot of us secretly struggle with fulfilling. No, I'm not referring to loving others, although there are some special kind of people who like to make that commandment extra challenging on certain days...like Mondays.

I digress.

The universal purpose we all have is to fulfill the great commission.

———————❋———————

Therefore, go and make disciples of all the nations, baptizing them in the name of the Father and the Son and the Holy Spirit. (Matthew 28:19).

———————❋———————

I don't want to assume that just because you are reading this book that you know what salvation is or why we need it. Listen, I was in church for years and I didn't realize the significance of Jesus dying until I was in my early 20s.

To fully understand the importance of fulfilling the great commission, we must first understand what exactly the great commission *is*. The great commission is the charge to share the Good News of salvation through Jesus Christ. In other words, we are to tell people of how God sent His Son, Jesus, to die for our sins and redeem mankind back to Him (John 3:15-18).

Now ask yourself this question without any judgment attached to it: Do you feel confident that you would be able to effectively articulate to someone why they need salvation? If the answer is *yes*, then awesome sauce! If the answer is no, my goal is to provide you with the answers, supported by scripture, to fully equip you with the knowledge necessary for you to be confident to lead someone to salvation.

Alright, let's break it down!

The Fall

Before we can fully comprehend the importance of salvation, we must first know why we need a Savior. To best understand this, we must tackle this subject from the beginning. When you study the book of Genesis, you will learn that God created man in His own image, starting with Adam (Genesis 1:27; Genesis 2:7). After he was formed, Adam's purpose was to tend to and watch over the Garden of Eden (Genesis 2:15). Within the garden, God placed the Tree of Life and the Tree of the Knowledge of Good and Evil (Genesis 2:9). He told Adam, "You may freely eat the fruit of every tree in the garden— except the tree of the knowledge of good and evil. If you eat its fruit, you are sure to die" (Genesis 2:16-17).

Now fast-forward to Eve. After God formed her out of Adam's rib, we find her having a conversation with a serpent in the garden (Genesis 3:1-5). Take into consideration that prior to the fall, snakes did not have a negative reputation as they do with us now, so Eve didn't have a reason to be afraid or cautious when she encountered it (Genesis 3:14-15).

From the context of the scripture, we can assume that Satan disguised himself as the serpent. After talking with Eve, he convinced her to eat the fruit that God instructed Adam not to (Genesis 3:1-7). She then gave the fruit to her husband, who I just want to point out, "was with her" (Genesis 3:6).

This is why it is so important to have a man who truly takes heed and obeys what God instructed *him* to do. You better make sure that the man you marry loves and listens to God more than He does to you. As his wife, you could unintentionally be a hindrance to him by giving him something or saying something, that appears to be good when it's really deception wrapped in an appealing package.

Notice that sin didn't enter the world until Adam ate the fruit—not Eve. Even though she knew she wasn't supposed to eat the fruit either, the instruction by God was given to Adam. I'm just going to leave that little tidbit there to marinate.

After they ate the fruit, Adam and Eve realized they were naked. Then, they attempted to hide themselves from God (Genesis 3:7-10). Due to their disobedience, God told Eve, "I will sharpen the pain of your pregnancy, and in pain you will give birth. And you will desire to control your husband, but he will rule over you" (Genesis 3:16). This gives us insight as to why wives are to submit to their husbands, as it established order after the fall.

I'm not even going to address the fact that this is the culprit of women having to endure excruciating labor pains. I'm just going to insert a sarcastic "thanks sis" as we collectively side eye Eve.

Oh, but don't you worry. Adam had his own set of consequences. God told him:

The ground is cursed because of you. All your life you will struggle to scratch a living from it. It will grow thorns and thistles for you, though you will eat of its grains. By the sweat of your brow will you have food to eat until you return to the ground from which you were made (Genesis 3:17-19).

From there, Adam and Eve were banished from the Garden of Eden (Genesis 3:23-24). I know you might be thinking, "Jeez that seems so harsh! What a mean God," but just follow me for a minute.

When Adam and Eve lived in the Garden of Eden, it was similar to being in heaven. It was perfect; there was no sin, and they walked freely with the Lord. If they would have remained in the garden after they disobeyed God, and continued to eat from the tree of life, they would have lived forever (Genesis 3:22). The problem with this is that they wouldn't have had eternal life in the perfect state that they did prior to the fall. Instead, they would have lived in an eternal state of sin.

Remember what their response was after they disobeyed God? They hid themselves. So, imagine being in a constant state of hiding from God because of the shame attached to sin. That was never the type of relationship that God wanted to have with His people. He created us to be in fellowship with Him, but sin resulted in us being separated from Him. Therefore, measures had to be put in place in an attempt to reconcile people back to God.

After the Fall

After sin entered the world, people would offer a sacrifice, known as a burnt offering, to the Lord to make atonement, or amends, for their sins. The burnt offering had to be a male animal without any imperfections and it was slaughtered on an altar that was dedicated to the Lord (Leviticus 1:1-17). The significance of this is that Romans 6:23 tells us that the payment for sin is death. Therefore, prior to Jesus' death and resurrection, the sacrifice of the dead animal acted as a substitute for the punishment that a person otherwise should have received for their sin (Leviticus 1:4).

In addition to this, people also had to depend on a third party to atone for their sins. This was done through the Jewish Custom called the Day of Atonement. It was designated as a day for the mourning and repentance of Israel's sins and it took place once per year. At this time, the high priest would go to the temple to make amends for the sins of the nation (Exodus 30:10; Leviticus 16:1-34; Hebrews 9:7). Within the temple of Jerusalem, there were the courts and two sacred rooms known as the Holy Place and the Most Holy Place, which were both separated by a veil (Exodus 26:33).

In the Most Holy Place was the Ark of the Covenant. It was made of acacia wood and it was covered, both inside and out, with pure gold (Exodus 25:10-11). Inside of the Ark were the Ten Commandments, and there was a special cover over it called the Mercy Seat (Exodus 25:17). This was known as the atonement cover, and it was where the Lord's presence rested (Exodus 25:21-22). The high priest was the only one who could enter the Most Holy Place and he was only allowed to do so once a year. To say that sin changed the relationship status with God to "it's complicated," would have been an understatement.

Jesus Redeems the World

No matter how many burnt offerings were presented to God, there was never a sacrifice pure enough to reconcile people back to their rightful position with Him (Hebrew 10:1-18). God the Father sent His Son, Jesus, to the earth in the womb of the virgin Mary, to redeem mankind once and for all (Matthew 1:18-25). Jesus was the perfect sacrifice because He had no sin, yet He died for the sins of people (2 Corinthians 5:21). He paid the debt in full that we could've never paid ourselves. Not only that, God sent Him to pay this debt for us, while we were yet still sinners (Romans 5:8).

But He was pierced for our rebellion, crushed for our sins. He was beaten so we could be whole. He was whipped so we could be healed (Isaiah 53:5).

Before He was nailed to the cross, He was beaten, whipped, taunted, and a crown of thorns was placed on His head (Matthew 27:15-44; Mark 15:6-20; Luke: 13-43; John 19:1-27). Once Jesus died, the veil in the temple was completely torn, which symbolized that people would now have access to God through the sacrifice of Christ (Matthew 27:51). They no longer had to present a burnt offering or have the high priest make amends for them, because Jesus was the perfect sacrifice that reconciled all of mankind back to the Father.

Now don't get it twisted. The fact that Jesus died was necessary, but it's not the only important factor. It's also the fact that He defeated death when God raised Him from the dead, three days later that truly sealed the deal (Matthew 28:1-20). When He rose from the grave, it showed God's divine power and affirmed that Jesus truly was the Son of God. It also validated His claim that He would be resurrected three days later (Mark 8:31; Mark 9:31, Mark 10:34; John 2:19).

We can believe by faith that the same power that raised Jesus from the dead is available to us through the Holy Spirit (Romans 8:11). As a result of this, we have the guarantee that those who believe in Jesus Christ as the Son of God will be resurrected when He returns and spend eternity with the Lord (1 Thessalonians 13-18; John 11:25-26; Romans 6:5-11; 1 Corinthians 15: 21-23).

I gave you this in-depth background information to make sure that you have a clear understanding of the gospel. Keep in mind, however, that when you're talking to someone who you either don't have much time with or who doesn't know much about the Bible, there is a such thing as information overload. Simply give them the basics.

Adam and Eve were kicked out of the Garden of Eden after they disobeyed God and caused sin to enter the world. Because of this, people were separated from God and they attempted to make atonement for their sins by offering burnt sacrifices to Him. The issue with this was that the blood that was sacrificed was never pure enough to reconcile people back with God. Therefore, He sent His Son, Jesus, as the perfect sacrifice to die for the sins of man and to redeem us back to God. After He died, God raised Jesus from the dead three days later. The importance of this is that we won't die in our sin and face eternal damnation, but instead we have everlasting life in heaven with the Lord. Likewise, we're able to presently live in freedom and abundance as we trust by faith the return of Jesus Christ.

Boom!

Now that we have the basics covered, let's talk about, well...why we don't talk about it! For every action, or lack thereof, there's always a root attached to it. Until you identify the root of where your actions stem from, you'll only scratch the surface of the issue but you'll never actually resolve it for good. That being said, many people fail to share the gospel. Rather than simply encouraging people to share it, we must first identify the root issue from which this common lack of action stems from. Let's discuss a few reasons why believers struggle with sharing the Good News with others!

1. They don't know how to effectively witness, or they don't feel comfortable witnessing.

Is it just me, or does it seem like our voice goes up an octave or five when we start talking to someone about Jesus? We can be having a normal conversation, but when the topic shifts to religion, something just changes in our posture, tone, demeanor, eyebrows, and everything. We get nervous and our focus shifts from leading a person to Christ to wondering if we're saying the rights things. You never want to miss the opportunity to lead someone to Christ because you feel like you don't know how to. So, we're going to go ahead and get rid of that excuse today!

If a person asks you what they need to do to be saved, you should be able to lead them to Romans 10:9-10:

> *If you confess with your mouth that Jesus is Lord and believe in your heart that God raised Him from the dead, you will be saved. For it is by believing in your heart that you are made right with God, and it is by openly declaring your faith that you are saved.*

That Biblical promise is a great place to start. Now obviously, there are many more things that you can discuss, such as repentance and baptism, but keep in mind that you don't want to overload a person with information. When people get overwhelmed, they tend to shut down and think that it's too much. Give them the basics and try to get them plugged into a solid, Bible-teaching church where they can be taught the Word of God.

Notice I suggested talking to them about church *after* you talk to them about salvation. Oftentimes people confuse inviting a person to church with making disciples and winning souls for Christ. Understand that although they are both important, they are not exclusively the same. You can invite a person to church who will never go on to get saved or even hear about salvation. In contrast, if you talk to a person about salvation and lead them to Christ, they're more likely to get plugged into a church as a result of accepting salvation.

Peter gives us a great example of this in Acts chapter 2 when he witnesses to a large group of people on the day of Pentecost, a traditional Jewish festival. After a group of believers were filled with the Holy Spirit, they began speaking in each other's languages. A crowd of people overheard them and accused them of being drunk (Acts 2:1-13). Peter approached the crowd and he began sharing the gospel with them. If you read the remainder of chapter 2, there are three key factors that you can take away from this example of witnessing:

- Peter acknowledged that Jesus died and that God raised Him from the dead (Acts 2:32).
- He told the crowd that Jesus is the Messiah (Acts 2:36).
- He instructed them to repent of their sins, turn to God, be baptized in the name of Jesus Christ, and receive the gift of the Holy Spirit (Acts 2:38).

We then learn that, "those who believed what Peter said were baptized and added to the church that day— about 3,000 in all" (Acts 2:41). They were added to the church *after* Peter talked to them about who Jesus was,

17

repentance, and the Holy Spirit. He didn't simply invite them to church and hope they'd figure it out there.

Finally, follow-up is so important! If you can keep in touch with the person, do so. Don't assume that just because they gave their life to Christ, they will stay in the faith. I don't know about you, but when I first got saved it was HARD. After being saved for the last eight years, guess what? It is still very hard sometimes!

Don't hesitate to ask people how they are genuinely doing. People backslide more often than you may think. Life happens, and people's faith begins to waver. Don't assume that they're fine; actually check in and follow up. It's always great to have encouragement, support, and accountability in this walk, so if you're able to offer it, then do so.

2. They fear that they don't know enough to answer a person's questions.

It's perfectly okay to say that you don't know something! I don't know why we have an inner inkling that tries to convince us that we should have an answer for everything. It is better for you to say that you don't know than to give someone an answer that doesn't line up with scripture or that leads a person away from God. If you don't know, say you don't know! That's a great opportunity to invite them to a Bible study or to reconnect with them after you study the topic in the Bible.

With that being said, as a believer, there are a few basics that you must know. You have to know Romans 10:9. Just like you have to have Polynesian sauce when you order from Chick-fil-a, you also have to know Romans 10:9. You should be able to confidently lead someone to salvation as a believer. Why is this important? What if someone wants to accept salvation and your pastor isn't around? There's no one there but you and that person, and the next service at church that you want to invite them to is five days away. What if they don't want to go to church but they want to accept salvation in that moment? What are you going to do? God forbid you wait for someone else to lead them to Christ and that person dies in their sin. I know this may seem like an extreme example, but it's a reality.

We should be able to lead people to salvation and effectively communicate to them why it is necessary. Consider what thoughts would go through your mind if someone told you that you needed to be saved but when you asked them why, their response was, "I don't know, that's what my momma said," or "Christian's just be doing stuff." If you don't know what you believe in or why you believe in it, how can you expect someone else to be receptive to it?

I cannot stress enough how important it is to understand the basics of salvation as a believer. Are all components of the Bible important and necessary as well? Absolutely! But in the grand scheme of things, the specifics on whether the fruit that Adam and Eve ate was an apple, blueberry, or watermelon, are irrelevant in comparison to salvation.

I must also add that it's important to study the Bible for yourself. Don't just accept what people quote or say about the Bible simply because they speak eloquently or have a title. Study the scriptures for yourself and allow the Bible to be your source.

Not what you think.

Not how you feel on Sundays.

Not your momma or auntie's traditions.

Not a devotional or a great sermon you listened to.

Not simply what you've heard your pastor say.

Allow the Bible to be your foundation. As you get an understanding of the basics of salvation, continue to seek God for wisdom in other areas of His word. James 1:5 tells us, "if you need wisdom, ask our generous God, and He will give it to you. He will not rebuke you for asking."

Furthermore, seek the Lord for discernment so that you're able to understand the type of person you are dealing with. A lot of times, people get nervous to witness to others because they're afraid that the person will start a debate with them and they won't know what to say. Understand that there are people who are sincere inquirers. They are the people who ask questions because they genuinely want to know. They're not trying to set you up for the okey-doke. On the other hand, you have people who want to debate, and they will ask you questions with a rebuttal already in mind. They want to pick apart what you believe in and they want to confuse you. Allow God to give you wisdom to discern the difference between the two, and respond accordingly.

If it brings you any comfort, know that there is not one person who knows absolutely everything about the Bible. The truth is, you can read the Bible from cover to cover and still not fully know or understand everything in it. It's possible to have knowledge of a topic, yet still lack wisdom in it. We should always remain teachable and in a position for God to continue to reveal new things to us through His Word. Don't allow an insecurity of not knowing enough to keep you from winning souls for Christ; none of us have it all figured out!

Even as I wrote this, there was a part of me that questioned if I was articulating it correctly.

Did I leave something out?

Would someone read this and disagree?

The truth is, I am an overthinker and one of my biggest frustrations is being misunderstood.

I've come to realize, and I still have to remind myself at times, that the Word of God will always speak for itself.

People can try to debate with you and twist and turn it to make it fit what they want it to, but at the end of the day, their personal beliefs do not change the Word of God.

3. They don't think it's their responsibility.

Lastly, some, if not many, believers think that leading people to Christ is solely the duty of their pastor and other leaders in the church. That's a lie from the pits of hell. Sharing the gospel is a charge to all who identify themselves as believers. Your pastor and other leadership, likely aren't at your job, around your family and friends, or the people who you encounter on a daily basis. God has placed *you* in your environment for you to reach and share the Good News with the people around you. Those people are assigned to you—not your pastor. Just because you invited your friend's, cousins, sister, to church with you, that doesn't put the responsibility on your pastor to lead them to salvation. It could very well be for you to lead them but instead of walking them through salvation, you just keep inviting them to church.

Consider this—when is the last time you heard a sermon strictly on salvation? If recently, that's great, and if not, that doesn't necessarily mean that your church isn't teaching sound doctrine. The reason I bring this up is because the first time a person hears the message of salvation, regarding what it is, why it's significant, and why they need to be saved, will likely not be during a

Sunday service. Do churches have a call for salvation at the end of their sermons? Yeah, many do. But opening the altar for someone to accept salvation is typically a brief moment where Romans 10:9 is quoted and then people praise or shout over their new brother or sister in Christ.

Then what?

They confessed with their mouth that Jesus is Lord and that God raised Him from the dead three days later, but do they know *why* He had to die? Do they understand the significance of God raising Jesus from the dead?

I know that there are new member classes, pamphlets, and all that great stuff, but keep in mind that those are resources that usually only reach the people who make it to a church and who choose to continue to attend. Therefore, it's important as a believer to be proactive in the environment that we've been placed in to win souls for Christ.

Obviously, this is not an all-inclusive list; it's simply a starting point. A starting point to get you thinking and to start a conversation. Just because your "why" wasn't listed, that doesn't mean it doesn't exist. If you profess to be a believer but you don't talk to anyone about salvation, identify *why* you've failed to do so. This isn't to attack you or to make you feel like a *bad* follower of Christ. I simply want you to consider this because there's so much work to do for the kingdom of God. Whether you believe it or not, you play an instrumental role in that work being completed.

I'm reminded of when Jesus went throughout the synagogues teaching and performing miracles. As He saw the crowds of people, He had compassion for them as they were "like sheep without a shepherd" (Matthew 9:35-36). He turned to His disciples and said, "The harvest is great, but the workers are few. So, pray to the Lord who is in charge of the harvest; ask him to send more workers into his fields" (Matthew 37-38).

This word also applies to us today. There are people who want to know Jesus and who want to have a relationship with Him, but they're waiting for someone to show them the way. The need is present, but the workers are few. The desire is present, but the believers who are capable and willing to share the Good News of salvation through Jesus Christ are few. Are you willing to share Jesus with others or are you waiting for one of the few to step in and do what you're equipped to do? God needs you to be present and proactive in the field that He has placed you in because there are people within your reach who still need the Good News.

As I'm sharing this message with you, I'm also giving the same charge to myself. We can't remain comfortable with attending church, small groups, Bible studies, and immersing ourselves in Christian community yet completely avoiding the very heartbeat of Christ, which is making disciples.

Challenge: Have a conversation with at least one person this week about the Good News of salvation through Jesus Christ.

Chapter 2

Inadequacy

God, You Chose Wrong

➤➤➤➤➤ ———————— ⫷⫷⫷⫷⫷

Have you ever felt like God dialed the wrong number when He called you to fulfill a vision that seemed so farfetched? Maybe you tried to ignore it, but then you went up for an altar call and the prophet read your entire journal and confirmed what you were running from. It's as if you look at the calling on your life like it's a bill collector or someone you regret giving your number to.

You know what I'm talking about!

I mean that person who calls you all the time and you sit, phone in hand, as you watch it ring. That's how we tend to avoid God's call on our lives.

Let's be honest, occasionally the reason for this is laziness. Other times, however, it's because we feel inadequate to fulfill the very thing that God has purposed us for. You would be surprised by how many people attend church, read their Bibles, and have a relationship with God, yet struggle to feel adequate. They've been told that God has amazing plans for their life, they're purposed for this or that, and God has even given them a vision of the ways He intends to use them. However, it all gets shut down though by feelings of inadequacy.

I know that struggle all too well. I can't tell you how many times I've laid on my floor with the ugly cry face, looking like a scene out of a very dramatic Lifetime movie. There have been too many moments to count where I told God through incoherent tears that I didn't feel cut out for what He's called me to. I wish I could say that it was a one-time, wham-bam, thank you ma'am ordeal where I gave myself a super spiritual pep talk that got me together, but that's not the case.

There are days where I feel confident and excited to take on what God has called me to, and then there are days where I say, "God, You chose wrong with this one." I've told Him countless times that He could've chosen someone who was more disciplined, consistent, and faithful to do what He's called me to. He's shown me every time that yes, He *could* have, but He chose me. He's still very confident in His choice.

Do you know that God is confident in His choice in you, even when you are not?

It's easy to feel insecure, overwhelmed, and unworthy to accept what God has called you to. Truth be told, some of us wouldn't even choose ourselves for what God has chosen us for. We would respond just as Moses did and offer suggestions for other people who are way more cut out for the task (Exodus 4:13). Isn't it amazing how when God reveals someone else's purpose, we can be so supportive and encouraging to them, but when it comes to our purpose, we tend to start ragging on ourselves?

We will prepare an entire essay, accompanied by a PowerPoint slide with exhibits A through F as to why we are not the one for the assignment at hand. We'll tell God that our age hinders us, we don't know enough, we're not articulate, we're better in the background, we didn't come from a "religious" family, and the list goes on and on...and on. I can imagine God thinking, "Okay, are you finished? Because there's work to be done." Matter of fact, let's look at God's response to a few of our brother's rebuttals when He told them the plans He had for them.

When God informed our little brother Jeremiah that He set him apart to be a prophet to the nations, Jeremiah's immediate response was, "I can't speak for You, I'm too young!" (Jeremiah 1:5-6). Now I know it may be very tempting to roll your eyes at Jeremiah's response, but how many times have you heard someone say that they'll serve God when they're older? Perhaps even *you* said it yourself.

Some people feel inadequate because they don't believe they are mature enough or they worry that they won't be well-received because of their age. Then there's the other side where people who have gracefully aged feel as though they've missed their opportunity because they're older now.

Here's a reality check, none of those fears or concerns negate what God has called you to. He wasn't intimidated by these factors when He selected you according to His purpose. He doesn't look at it to be an issue because His focus is on a heart that is willing to obey and surrender to His instruction. God told Jeremiah to go where He led him and speak whatever He told him to (Jeremiah 1:7). He then promised that He would give him the words to speak and that He didn't have to be afraid of what people might say or do to him, because He would be with Jeremiah and He would protect him (Jeremiah 1:8-10).

Now, let's talk about brother Gideon. We meet Gideon in Judges 6, after we learn that the Israelites were being oppressed by the Midianites for seven years due to their disobedience (Judges 6:1-6). An angel appeared to Gideon and told him that the Lord was with him (Judges 6:12). Now Gideon's response was very much like ours when we are faced with all kinds of different tests and trials. He looks at the angel and says:

If the Lord is with us, why has all this happened to us? And where are all the miracles our ancestors told us about? Didn't they say the Lord brought us up out of Egypt? But now the Lord has abandoned us and handed us over to the Midianites (Judges 6:12-13).

Is it just me or do you sense the sass in Gideon's voice too?

I love that in the next verse, it is the Lord, not the angel, who tells Gideon, "Go with the strength you have and rescue Israel from the Midianites. I am sending you" (Judges 6:14). Gideon's tone changed when he realized that he would be the appointed one to change the condition of the Israelites. He responds with, "But Lord, how can I rescue Israel? My clan is the weakest in the whole tribe of Manasseh, and I am the least in my entire family" (Judges 6:15).

Did you catch the irony?

God told Gideon to go with the strength that he already had, but Gideon focused on the weakness that he perceived he had. God knew that Gideon could handle the task He had given him because God had already provided Gideon with the strength to do it.

I can imagine that Gideon probably didn't feel strong because of the circumstances surrounding him and the Israelites. In the same way, in your life, feelings of inadequacy may sink in as you look at your brokenness and what is falling apart in your life, which convinces you that God has left you. You don't feel like He can use you because your life is in shambles. You don't have any strength left to push forward because you feel beat down and defeated. It's easy to be consumed by inadequacy when you focus on your limitations versus God's strength. You won't know what strength you possess in the Lord until you start exercising it.

Finally, let's look at someone who made multiple attempts to get out of what God called him to. If you guessed Mr. Moses, then you are right!

When God first told Moses that He would use him to deliver the Israelites out of bondage in Egypt, Moses protested, "Who am I?" (Exodus 3:11) He protested to God! That means he was openly objecting and showing disapproval of what God had instructed him to do. That's pretty gutsy Mo Mo. Despite this, God tells Moses that He will be with him and even gives him a sign that He is the one who sent him (Exodus 3:12).

Moses still tries to find a way to get out of being obedient by telling God that the people would question who sent him. But God says, tell them "I Am Who I Am" (Exodus 3:13-14).

Whelp, there you have it!

Moses wasn't done though; he gives another rebuttal as he tells God that he doesn't think that the people will believe him or listen to him (Exodus 4:1). God tells Moses to take his staff and throw it on the ground, and it turned into a snake. When he grabbed the tail of the snake, it turned back into his staff. God informed Moses that this would be the sign that He had appeared to him, and that God was the one who sent him (Exodus 4:2-5).

Moses still wasn't ready to let up. He goes on to tell God that he's not an articulate man, therefore he clearly wouldn't make a great mouthpiece for Him (Exodus 4:10).

I just want to point out that for someone who swore they weren't good with words, he sure did put in a lot of work attempting to talk himself out of what God told him to do.

Nonetheless, God told Moses that He is who created the mouth and that He would be with him and tell him what to say (Exodus 4:11-12). Moses makes one more attempt to get out of his assignment, but this time he doesn't even give an excuse, he just says, "Lord, please! Send anyone else" (Exodus 4:13). My inner introverted self connects with the desperation in his plea.

I feel you, Moses. I get it.

But God wasn't having it. Although He allowed Moses' brother, Aaron, to speak to the people for him, God still required Moses to do what He had called him to.

Maybe you feel inadequate like Moses because you're anticipating issues that you think you will run into. Or maybe you're afraid to do it by yourself. You don't feel like you'll be able to handle such a task; in focusing on that, you miss all the resources that God has equipped you with. As you're worried about things that may never even happen, you forget that He's not calling you to an assignment for you to do it alone or figure it out by yourself.

In case you missed it, let me point out the one common denominator between all three of these men. God called them and He told them that He would be with them. He says this as He reaffirms the assignment He has called them to. Notice, He never tells any of them, "when you get yourself together, then I'll be with you and use you." If that were the case, then no one would ever get anything done, yet alone even start! He doesn't need us to be self-assured or self-reliant to complete the job. He simply needs us to be confident in who He is and who we are in Him.

Every time you place your confidence in what you feel you're capable of handling, you'll end up missing out on fully seeing God's glory revealed in your life. At some point, you will realize that what you feel is not always indicative of who you are or your capabilities in God. When you learn to remove feelings out of the picture, you'll quickly see that you don't always have to *feel* called to be called. You don't always have to look the part to be set apart for the purpose that God has called you to.

You may not realize this, but trust and believe that Satan does. He will use your feelings of inadequacy to attack your confidence because there is true freedom and power that comes with walking boldly in who God created you to be. If the enemy can plant seeds in your mind to sift your confidence, he knows that it won't just affect you, but it will also have an impact on the people who God has assigned to you—those who you will ultimately end up missing by not being in your rightful position.

When we find ourselves feeling inadequate, we should ask, "What is the root of it?" What is the underlying reason behind why we feel that we are not sufficient to fulfill the very promise that God has on our lives? Sometimes the issue is a result of us trying to obtain a level of perfection in our own strength when we will never be able to do what God has appointed us to without completely relying on Him. In 2 Corinthians 12:9, Apostle Paul speaks directly to this as he talks about the thorn in his flesh that he prayed for God to remove.

Although Paul was an anointed man of God, he had an infirmity, his thorn, that he could not get rid of. He had a very close relationship with the Lord and he was very knowledgeable of the Word of God, yet he had this issue that he could not shake. Paul asked God three times to remove it and His response was, "My grace is sufficient for thee: for My strength is made perfect in weakness" (KJV).

Is it just me, or do you feel your help coming on, too?

A component of struggling with inadequacy is feeling insufficient. Do you realize that where you feel insufficient, God says, *My grace is sufficient?* Where you feel you are lacking something that is essential to you being perfect or fit to fulfill the assignment that He has given to you, He says, *My strength is made perfect in weakness.* He's telling you that where you lack, He resides.

Where you are full, He is sufficient.

Where you lack, He is sufficient.

Where you have abundance, He is *still* sufficient.

I need you to catch this!

God is enough; you don't have to worry about being good enough, you simply just have to *be.* Be who He created you to be. Be who He has called you to be. Be who He already predestined you to be. By you simply being, you are adequately equipped for your purpose.

The real question is, do you know who you are in Him and what He's called you to? Some people find it difficult to walk in who God has called them to be because they have a mistaken identity. They end up mistaking what other people labeled them as to be their true identity when it's not even close to who God created them to be. They conformed to their parent's, teacher's, friend's, supervisor's, and whoever else's version of them.

Since so and so said they would never amount to anything, they didn't have the skill, they weren't smart enough, pretty enough, or good enough, many people believe those words. They take on the identity of being the shy, quiet, passive one because that's what everyone labeled them as. Many begin to believe that there's no way they could be a mouthpiece for God. There's no way that they could stand before people and proclaim the gospel of Jesus Christ. According to the identity that they have been walking in, they don't fit the criteria or look the part.

That's how I've been viewed—too quiet, too timid, too young, and too whatever else to be in the position that I'm in. That was what I believed, too, for a moment. I was always the little quiet one in the background. I struggled with figuring out what it meant and looked like to be a woman in ministry. I didn't fit the mold and therefore I felt very unsure of what God called me to. I didn't *look* like a minister. I loved a good red lip and I still do. I got way too many tattoos before I was saved and I can't always cover them. I'm not down for wearing stockings in the heat of the summer. It's just not going to happen. But I love Jesus with all my heart. I want to fulfill God's will for my life and I'm so thankful that He doesn't choose us based on people's narrow perceptions of what they assume we are or are not capable of.

When feelings of inadequacy attempt to creep into your mind, you have to speak life. Remind yourself of who you are in God and what His Word says about you. If you need to write it out, write it down in a journal or on sticky notes and place it somewhere that it is visible. If you want to look in the mirror and remind yourself that you are called and chosen when you don't feel so, do it. If you must stand, or kneel, with arms stretched and say, "I am the head and not the tail," say it (Deuteronomy 28:13).

Speak it boldly!

"I am who God says that I am. I am gifted, anointed, and called for such a time as this. I will fulfill the will of God in my life and I believe that He will supply all my needs according to His riches and glory (Philippians 4:19). I am chosen, a royal priesthood, a holy nation, and God's very own possession (1 Peter 2:9). I will bear good fruit for the kingdom of God and I will walk in purpose, and on purpose. I am a child of God. Because of that I have purpose and no devil in hell will keep me from fulfilling it. I am God's masterpiece, created to perform good works and it shall be fulfilled" (Ephesians 2:10).

Repeat it as often as you need to.

Declare it.

Decree it.

Believe it.

Chapter 3
Comparison
But She Isn't Even Trying to Live for God

‑»»)))))———————————((((((«‑

I was sitting in the drive thru at Wendy's when I felt the knot in my throat and the burning sensation in my nose, informing me that I could not hold back the waterfall of tears that were getting ready to take place. I was hoping that the cashier would hand me my nuggets and junior bacon cheeseburger at any moment, because I didn't know how much longer I could hold it in. The last thing I needed was this teenage boy thinking that I was crying over waiting for food.

When he came to the window, I grabbed my bag, smiled and said, "thank you," as I felt a tear roll down my cheek. I drove off with this poor kid looking at me as I'm convinced he was thinking, "Stay crazy, lady." As soon as the waterworks began, I sighed in frustration and said, "She isn't even trying to live for You, God!"

Ooh, that's ugly, right?

I was in my feelings because I was looking at someone else who appeared to be getting blessed in all these different areas. She had just moved into a new apartment. She was in a happy relationship. She had a job that she actually loved and enjoyed. Not only was everything working out for her, but when it came to the things I was believing God for, she got them.

How?

Why?

No, seriously how?

It was evident from her lifestyle that she was not trying to live for God none whatsoever. I didn't understand how she was over there prospering while I was being promoted to first class on the struggle bus. I was frustrated because I did not get it!

You might be thinking that the Lord eventually revealed to me that just because it appeared she was being blessed, it didn't mean that she was. Or that He showed me how Satan was setting traps through what appeared to be blessings. All that sounds cute, but He showed me none of that. Matter of fact, He never revealed anything to me about her. He didn't need to because she wasn't the source of my problem; my heart was.

I needed to deal with the fact that I had allowed comparison to take root in my life. Not only did I allow it, but I also watered the seeds of jealousy, envy, and discontentment as they blossomed from what I failed to uproot.

The comparison game is such a sneaky little cycle. It will have you distracted and discontent as you focus on everyone else. You'll find yourself looking at someone else's life with a slight, or maybe even major, side-eye as you wonder how they ended up in the position they are in. This is especially the case when you think that they aren't making any attempts to obey God, yet alone serve Him in any capacity.

Meanwhile, you've been abstaining for years, serving in different ministries, loving Jesus, minding your business, and drinking water but you're just as single as they come. On the other hand, sister busted and disgusted always has a man and is on her third engagement, while you can't even get a text back. As you scroll through social media, you're convinced that everyone is living their best life ever.

Everyone except for you, that is.

People are traveling and living it up while you're trying to calculate whether you'll run out of money before your next paycheck. It seems like everyone is being promoted, starting businesses, moving, expanding their families, and it feels like you've been left behind and overlooked. You find yourself frustrated because you're trying to do the right things and it appears that everyone who is doing wrong is winning.

Comparison always emphasizes what you lack by leading you to overlook everything that you already possess. It's the breeding ground for a jealous, envious, and covetous attitude that can lead you to become discontent with your portion and ultimately become self-destructive. It can even lead you to a point where you're bitter and upset with a person who you don't even know, or, wait for it...who doesn't know you.

I remember following a beauty guru on Instagram. Every time I saw her pictures, I found myself getting in my feelings. She was stunning and she always had cute outfits, perfectly slayed hair, and her makeup stayed on point. In addition to this, home girl was thicker than a snicker and I've been the president and CEO of the sweet petite crew since I came out of the womb. When I looked at her pictures, I would find myself feeling insecure about the fact that I weigh about the same as an overweight toddler, even on my best day. I eventually became super critical of what she posted as I rolled my eyes and thought about how tight her clothes were, or how she should have done her hair differently.

First and foremost, I'm painfully aware now that it's never that serious. Secondly, the girl was gorgeous and me being a hater wasn't going to change that. I had to acknowledge that my issues weren't with her, but they were with myself. As someone who has struggled with body image issues, looking at her reminded me of what I lacked, yet very much so desired to have. When I compared my lack of va-va-voom to her "body-ody," it was easy to feel insecure about an area that was already a soft spot for me. Who she was, what she posted, and how she looked was not what triggered my response. It was my inability, or refusal even, to acknowledge and deal with my insecurities and heart issues.

When you're struggling with comparison, it's easy to focus on everyone else while never quite examining why you feel the way you do. You'll end up dismissing signs of the issue because you don't want to deal with the reality of it. When you do the work that leads you to the root of comparison, it is not going to be easy. It will require you to dig deep and address things about yourself that you've suppressed or just don't want to deal with. It's not going to be one of those, "God, I just be doing stuff" conversations. No ma'am! God likes to heal us at the root and not just the surface-level issues that we tend to bring Him. He's going to deal with the why's, what's, who's, and how's to fully enable us to experience freedom from comparison.

To walk in that freedom, you'll have to acknowledge what the issue is. It's easy to dismiss what you don't want to see, but accepting it enables you to do something about it. Initially, you may not recognize that comparison is the real issue because it's masked under other behaviors that you may disregard. Maybe you find yourself feeling inadequate or constantly jealous or envious of others. Or you tend to be judgmental or very critical as you people-watch or scroll through your timelines.

Perhaps you find it difficult to genuinely be happy for someone else's success because it didn't happen to you. Maybe you were always compared to your siblings or classmates when you were younger, and it impacted how you view yourself in relation to others as an adult. You now focus on what you lack by always relating it to what someone else has.

Here's the thing: we live in such a goals-oriented world, where it's very easy to get consumed with what everyone else is doing in comparison to us. There are "goals" for everything nowadays! Relationship goals, house goals, eyebrow goals, you name it, it's goals. People are in constant competition as they try to be the best and outdo the rest. The world continues to convince us that there is only one way to define beauty, one way to measure success, one deadline for marriage and children, and so on. When you find yourself outside of what has been predefined as "the way," you end up focusing on what you lack instead of what God has already provided. While you look at everyone else's life in comparison to yours, you miss what God desires to do in you.

Instead of embracing who God created you to be, you look at other people who appear to have it together and label them as goals. Even within the church, we have allowed people with titles, platforms, and a word to become goals for us. We've made idols out of people and their ministries as we hide behind the claims of supporting them, yet not realizing that we're more loyal to them than we are to God. Some have even deceived themselves into thinking that they're following Christ because they're supporting a ministry, all while it's really more about following the person. Listen, there's nothing wrong with having goals or having people that you look to as an example to achieve that goal. The issue arises, however, when the goal or the person, becomes your standard instead of Christ.

Apostle Paul even told people to follow him as he follows Christ (1 Corinthians 11:1). If he chose to turn to sin, the people following him shouldn't have been impacted by it to the extent that they too would turn away from the faith, just because their leader fell. When we start looking at people to be our example, it becomes easy to view their life as the model for Christian living instead of seeking God and reading His Word. As we compare our walk with Christ to theirs, we can make the mistake of adapting to their personal convictions or traditions and substituting it for the Bible. We can also disregard our own convictions simply because we see that other Christians can do what God clearly told us not to.

I used to love to watch the show *Scandal*. I was a full-on gladiator at heart and I was here for all things Olivia Pope. As I grew in my walk with Christ, I started to get convicted about watching the show that I loved so much. When I would check Twitter, I would see tons of people talking about their favorite parts from the episode airing, and a lot of them were self-proclaimed Christians. I figured that if other believers were watching it, then there clearly was nothing wrong with me watching it too, right?

Wrong!

I didn't know if God convicted them about watching the show, and quite frankly it was irrelevant to what I did know. I knew that God told me no; period and the end. It didn't matter if everybody else could watch it because He had convicted me not to. He had to be my standard, not other believers.

When the body of Christ falls into the trap of comparing our walk with others, we can find ourselves seeking the advice of a person over Christ. Instead of becoming more like Him, we begin to mold ourselves into our favorite preachers and worship singers. We will quickly run to their conferences and watch their sermons with eagerness, yet hesitate to get out of our seat for an altar call or groan at the thought of studying our Bible. On the other hand, we find ourselves feeling inadequate as we look at their perfectly-posted scriptures and blossoming ministries, as we wish that we had the type of relationship with God that they do.

Too often, believers make the mistake of comparing their relationship with God to others, when they have no idea how that person developed such a relationship. When you look at a person and admire how passionate and on fire for God they are, consider the fact that you likely don't know what sparked that fire. You don't see the private moments that they endured that birthed that passion. You don't see that it came with a price. You may never see the many tears that are shed, the sacrifices that are made, or the stripping and pruning seasons that drew them close to God. There will be things that they endure in private that you will never know about. It's not because they want people to think that everything is perfect; not at all. Sometimes God will take you through tests and

47

trials privately, because not everyone can handle the truth about your valley moments.

You see, everyone wants to have an intimate relationship with the Lord, but very few are willing to be disciplined and put in the work to get there. Even less are willing to endure through the various tests and trials that will really draw them closer to Christ.

I've learned to not covet or be envious of other's gifts and callings because I know it comes with a price. I know this because I know what it cost, and continues to cost, me. I could choose to sit and look at other people's ministries that are flourishing, bigger, and more successful in comparison to mine. I could focus on how others have more support and become discontent with what God has given me in my ministry, Changed Hearts.

I *could* do that.

Or I could accept the reality that I couldn't handle someone else's ministry. I'm not equipped to run Prophetess Hallelujah's ministry of 500,000 amazing women. It's not because I'm not good enough or that there's something wrong with me. It's simply that I am qualified for the assignment that God has entrusted *me* with, and comparing it to others only robs me of the fulfillment of accomplishing what I'm already equipped for.

The comparison seed is never planted with good intent. It's always a distraction. Its purpose is to cause confusion and to get our focus off what we should be doing. We must be mindful of how Satan will use comparison as a snare to distract us, not only from our purpose but to also create competition within the body of Christ. You might be thinking, "say it isn't so" as you clutch your pearls, but it's so girl!

Think about how many times you or someone you know looked at someone in ministry and thought that you could do a better job than they're doing. You could host bigger conferences and have a larger turnout because you feel like you *deserve* to for all your sacrifices. Or maybe you get annoyed with the woman who is in her birthing season; you're tired of her making announcements. You feel like she's doing too much and you're frustrated that she's doing the things that you wanted to do. Instead of viewing it as confirmation or being on one accord, you're mad because you didn't get to do it first. Now you're looking at others and wondering, "how did she get a title? How did she get called into ministry? Why did she get a husband before me?"

I mean this in the most respectful way ever...

WHO CARES?!

Why are you bitter, sis?

If that's what God has called her to, you should support her. Pray for her instead of talking about what you feel you could do better. That type of attitude is exactly how comparison and competition can be used to cripple the body of Christ. I don't know about you, but I don't want to be the reason why the body is limping or immobile.

We must realize that as the church, we are on the same team! The world shows you that there is one lane and you have to fight your way to the top to be the best or to be successful, but the Bible does not show us that. It tells us that we each have a role within the body of Christ, and each role is positioned to work together to bring people into the knowledge of salvation through Jesus Christ (1 Corinthians 12:12-31).

Apostle Paul breaks this down in 1 Corinthians chapter 12, as he explains that although there are different spiritual gifts and kinds of service, the source of them all is the Holy Spirit (1 Corinthians 12:4-6). Furthermore, the purpose behind there being different gifts and callings is so that we can help each other as the body (1 Corinthians 12:7). One gift is not superior to the other because they complement each other and should work in unity to build up the church. You may think that your role is insignificant in comparison to another part of the body, but it's necessary. Not only is it necessary, but

God Himself positioned you there to serve a purpose for the body (1 Corinthians 12:18).

Just because you don't stand behind the pulpit or lead worship, doesn't mean that the role you play isn't important. The fact that the foot can't do what the hand does doesn't make the foot less important than the hand. It makes it qualified to serve in the capacity that it was purposed and created for. Think about how crazy your body would look if your knee cap was in competition with your ear because it felt like it was better suited to help you hear, instead of realizing it best serves in helping you to walk. If your knee cap gets out of position, it will impact your body, which in return will affect its overall functionality. How much different do you think the impact is within the body of Christ?

As the church, we can't afford to be in competition with one another. We should all have the same goal of winning souls for Christ! We can't effectively attain that goal, however, when we're out of position within the body as we compare our role to our brother or sister. We're one body under Christ, so if your sister reaches someone who you didn't get over here, that's perfectly fine. You don't have to compare your reach to hers because at the end of the day, a soul was won and that's all that matters. Stick to your assignment. When you try to step into someone else's lane, you end up missing the people who God has led down your path. You miss what you're assigned to because you're busy trying to complete an assignment that you were never called to.

Know that you will never have to force or conform to what God has chosen you for. When you stop comparing your portion to others, you'll see that you're fully equipped to handle what He has for you. Don't be bound by comparison. It only prolongs you getting to where you desire to be in God. Be intentional about casting down every seed that it tries to plant. When the lies pop up that you know don't line up with who God says you are, trade it for the truth.

Most of the time, the lie isn't regarding the person who you're comparing yourself to; it's usually about you. It's those lies that tell you that you're inferior and that you don't have what it takes. It's the thoughts that you aren't good enough, liked enough, and just overall not enough. It's what comes to mind as you look at others and become consumed by what you feel you lack in comparison. Sometimes it's even a self-righteous thought that comes to mind.

You know what I'm talking about!

That thought when you look at someone else's success and feel like it should've been you because you're a better Christian or holier. Baby girl, don't forget that your righteousness on its best day is still like filthy rags to God (Isaiah 64:6). We all need His grace and mercy!

Cast down those thoughts that are contrary to the Word of God (2 Corinthians 10:5). When stuff starts to pop into your mind that you know is nonsense, shut that mess down pronto. The more you entertain it or allow it to linger, the more it will grow and become rooted in your heart and mind. Shut it down and replace it with His Word.

In order to do this, you must know what His Word says about who you are. When you understand who you are in God, you're less likely to fall into the trap of comparison because you realize that who He created others to be does not diminish the significance of who you are. When you're confident in who you are in God and become one with His word, Satan may tempt you, but you overcome.

Use Jesus for example. When Jesus was led into the wilderness by the Holy Spirit and Satan tempted Him for forty long days (Luke 4:1-13), every time the enemy tried to trick Jesus with his words, Jesus always responded with scripture. Jesus resisted the temptation not just because He knew the Word, but because He *was* the Word, and therefore He knew Himself (John 1:1-5). He knew what His purpose on earth was for and He didn't allow the tactics of the enemy to sidetrack Him from fulfilling it.

When we become confident in who we are, what God has purposed us for, and what His Word says, we are able to fight against the schemes of Satan. We're able to recognize the lies and exchange them for the truths that are found throughout the Bible. When comparison tries to seep into our thoughts, we know that there's nowhere in the Bible that says we should compare ourselves to one another. We can cast that thought down and ask God to help us not succumb to it.

Instead of getting in your feelings, genuinely pray for the person you're comparing yourself to and ask God to change your heart towards them. If you find yourself constantly struggling with comparing your life to someone else's, sometimes you need to disconnect to get yourself right. If it means fasting from social media, unfollowing people, or not watching certain shows, do you, honey! I had to unfollow the beauty guru for my own sanity, and once I got myself together, I was able to follow her again. I liked her content, but at the time I needed to deal with my insecurities so I needed to detach.

There's nothing wrong with that!

Don't allow pride to convince you that it's not an issue when you know good and well that jealousy and envy are knocking on your front door like they're the police. Go ahead and deal with it and know that as you pour it all out to God, He will receive it and affirm who you are in Him.

Chapter 4
Fear
I'm Scared, Now What?

➤➤➤➤➤➤ ────────────── ⫷⫷⫷⫷⫷⫷

I Sometimes avoid things when they get hard. No, really. I used to think my problem was procrastination, but I'm really just a big avoider. Whenever I have a lot to do or I'm feeling overwhelmed, I tend to shut down and put off dealing with it until I absolutely must. It's gotten a little better as I've gotten older; I'm convinced that the closer you get to 30, the better things get.

Nonetheless, if I can be honest, which is what we're here for, this issue at times flows over into my spiritual life, too. There have been moments where I avoided having quiet time to deal with my issues because I was anxious about them. Recently, I found myself struggling with fear and anxiety as God started to show me different things. A year after quitting my job by faith in November

2016, the Lord began to show me that it was time to transition back into the workforce. Not only would I be transitioning back to work, but I'd also be moving out of my apartment and leaving the city I had lived in for the last eleven years. I had to move back home and live with my parents at twenty-nine years old because I didn't have the finances to live on my own. To top it off, the Lord revealed to me in July 2017, that I had until the end of the year to leave my church.

I wanted to run and escape the thought of it all because it was just too much! It didn't make sense, and majority of what I felt led to do, I really wanted to say no to. When I finally sat before the Lord for some real unfiltered, candid, and messy quiet time, what came out of my mouth even caught me by surprise.

God, I'm scared.

Along with tears and snot, those were the first words to come out. I had been avoiding the fact that I didn't feel comfortable with this plan that God had sprung on me. I had to deal with my truth and acknowledge that I wasn't on board with this transition. I didn't like the direction that God was leading me, and fear played a major role in that. I was afraid of what I couldn't understand because it didn't look like the plan I had already created for myself.

It's perfectly okay and necessary to cut to the chase and start with the real. Sometimes we can feel like we should pretty up our issues or present them in a way that makes us feel better about things we've disregarded. Especially when we're in a position where we know better and should do better.

I know the Bible tells us that God has not given us a spirit of fear, however, I was afraid (2 Timothy 1:7). What I knew (God's plans are good) conflicted with what I perceived (this isn't a good plan), based on how I felt (this doesn't feel good). We often don't recognize how our own perception can have a direct impact on how fear plays out in our life.

Fear is defined as "a distressing emotion aroused by impending danger, evil, pain, etc., whether the threat is real or imagined.[1]" I really hope you caught on to the game-changer in the latter part of that definition. It lets us know that although fear is a very real emotion, what causes that emotion may not necessarily be. Satan is hoping that you miss that key factor. He likes to plant seeds of fear, even when the fear is based on lies. He realizes that if he can get you to perceive that you should be afraid of failing or that people will reject you, it will keep you from even starting. You'll end up aborting the entire vision over the fear of something that may never even happen.

Isn't it amazing how we can know that God has placed this amazing anointing on our lives, but instead of operating in the calling, we choose to operate in fear? It's as if we have more faith in our ability to fail than who God created us to be. It's important to understand that just because fear is present, it doesn't mean the cause of the fear actually exists.

Think about it like this, if you were to walk outside with the intention of getting in your car and you see a bear looking at you like "what's good?" it would be a normal response to be afraid. The threat of danger is very real and present, so it's a natural reaction for fear to take over. But that's not the type of fear that a lot of people are walking in. They're walking in a perception of fear instead of the reality of fear. They have perceived that they won't be able to complete the task, it won't work out, or they're going to face opposition, so they don't even consider doing it. Mind you, nothing has happened yet for them to be afraid, but because they perceive there to be the threat of failing, being judged, etc., fear leads them to quit.

How many times have you talked yourself out of something that God instructed you to do, due to fear? Maybe He told you to write a blog, start a ministry or a business, go back to school, or quit your job and all you can do is think of all the reasons why it wouldn't work.

Perhaps you're more afraid of it working because it'd be easier to not have to commit or deal with everything that would be attached to it. You allow fear and doubt to talk you out of it as you focus on what you feel you are capable of, versus believing what God has called you to. Instead of turning to Him and allowing Him to affirm who He's called you to be, your feelings take over and you view His plan based on how you *feel* versus who you are in Him.

Don't you realize that this is exactly where Satan wants you to be? He knows that if he can instill fear in your heart before you even start, then you won't complete the task. If you don't start, then you won't get to the point where you're able to see that it will work out. You won't see that God is for you and that He's faithful to fulfill what He promised to you. The enemy tries to get you stuck in the perception of fear so that you will be convinced that you have a reason to be afraid of something that hasn't even happened yet.

It's crazy how we can spend so much time worrying about the "what if's" that we never even start. Instead of continuing to walk in whatever God has called us to, we allow the seed of fear and doubt to completely snatch and uproot the promises and vision that He placed in our heart. We then lose sight of the promise because our current season feels empty, nothing is working out, and it feels like brokenness will be our story forever. We're afraid that nothing is going to change and that this is how it will always be because this is how it has been for so long. We must realize that although it's a fact that seasons are temporary, it's false that temporary is equivalent to short. Don't allow a season that appears to be long and barren to convince you that God can't use even the driest of land and exchange it for fertile ground.

Take Joshua and the Israelites for example, as they journeyed through the wilderness for forty years before getting to the promised land (Joshua 5:6). Granted, it was their disobedience that prolonged them getting to their destination, but you can imagine that as time went on and as opposition came, they started to question what God had promised. He still showed Himself faithful, even when they were afraid and thought that it would've been better to remain in bondage in Egypt (Exodus 14:10-31). As He prepared Joshua to finally lead them into Canaan, He told him, "This is My command—be strong and courageous! Do not be afraid or discouraged. For the Lord your God is with you wherever you go" (Joshua 1:9).

I was having a Starbuck's date with a friend one day, and she talked about how the fact that God gave Joshua a command really hit her. We were looking at each other like, *wait a minute.* That was an instruction, not just a friendly reminder.

When we're struggling with fear, it's easy to encourage ourselves to be strong and courageous, but that isn't the most important part of this text. The key is that before God says any of that, He tells our friend, Josh, "This is My command." That means take heed, because what is said next is a directive. It's not just a good pick me up to say, nor is it simply a suggestion or recommendation. He *commanded* Joshua to be strong and courageous.

For a moment, I questioned, "Why?"

Then I imagined God replying as any great parent would with the infamous one-liner, "Because I said so!"

Well alright then.

Touché Lord, touché.

If we pay attention, however, we see that God answers the *why* multiple times. He tells Joshua to be strong and courageous two other times before He commands him to do so in verse nine. Each time God said this to Joshua it was right before He gave him instruction for his assignment.

Let's break it down right quick:

Command: *Be strong and courageous,* (Joshua 1:6)

Why: *for you are the one who will lead these people to possess all the land I swore to their ancestors I would give them* (Joshua 1:6).

Command: *Be strong and very courageous. Be careful to obey all the instructions Moses gave you. Do not deviate from them, turning either to the right or to the left. Then you will be successful in everything* (Joshua 1:7).

Why: God provided Joshua with all the tools he would need to succeed.

Command: *Be strong and courageous. Do not be afraid or discouraged* (Joshua 1:9).

Why: *For the Lord your God is with you wherever you go* (Joshua 1:9).

God told Joshua to not be afraid and to be strong and courageous because He knew Joshua was the person who could handle the assignment. He had provided him with all the tools necessary to be successful and He would be with him wherever he went. Now if He did it for our boy Jo Jo, what makes us think that we aren't also required to courageously enter into the place that God has called us to go?

Fear will try to tell you that you aren't cut out for it or that you will fail, but trust where God is leading you. He knows that you're the one to get the job done; do you? Do you not think that as God is giving you vision, instruction, and calling you out of your comfortable place, He doesn't already know that you're qualified to handle where He's leading you to next? Do you really think He would lead you somewhere to see you fail or to a place that He wouldn't go with you? He's given you His Word. With the Word, you have all the tools you need to be successful.

Be strong and courageous walking in the assignment that God has given you. The reason it is an instruction is because He already knows that you won't fail if you allow Him to lead the way. Completely surrender to His will today. Lay down your questions, worries, frustrations, doubts, and fears. Trust Him during the transition. Trust that He is a good Father, even when what you may be experiencing doesn't feel good. Trust that He will never lead you down a path that He hasn't already gone before you. He's assigned you to this task because He knows that you can handle it. He's prepared you, and now He needs you to walk boldly and courageously into this new season. This is what He equipped you for.

You can't afford to stay in a place that He has called you out of simply because it's comfortable. Too often people would rather stay in a place that is familiar, even though it is dysfunctional and not producing anything, simply because they fear the unknown. Step out and trust God's plans even when they don't make sense.

Yes, it will likely be hard. Yes, this may be the biggest sacrifice you've ever had to make. Yes, you may have questions, but just go. Go in faith and trust that He will be with you.

You might be thinking, "That sounds good, but how do I overcome fear when I don't feel bold and courageous?"

I'm so glad you asked!

In 2 Timothy 1:7, Apostle Paul tells Timothy that God hasn't given us a spirit of fear, but He has given us the Holy Spirit that helps us to operate in power, love, and self-discipline. Just to bring this into context, Timothy was facing opposition as a young leader for teaching the Good News of Jesus Christ. There was criticism from both believers and nonbelievers, and he had to deal with false prophets who were attempting to discredit his message. Paul was encouraging Timothy to not be intimidated or afraid of people or persecution, but instead to allow the Holy Spirit to work through him to complete his assignment.

When we find ourselves faced with fear concerning what God has called us to, we should be reminded that fear is not a manifestation of the Holy Spirit. In contrast, the Holy Spirit instills power that enables believers to be effective in fulfilling their mission. It's the same power that gives you authority over the enemy, to cast out demons, and to perform miracles (Luke 10:19; Luke 9:1; Mark 16:17-18). The Holy Spirit empowers you to love those who oppose and mistreat you, even when you would normally want to retaliate.

The Holy Spirit develops self-control within you to condition you to look more like Christ. He allows you to not be swayed by people, but to have the strength to stand on the true Word of God, despite opposition. Fear, on the other hand, convinces you that you're weak and timid so that you don't recognize the power you possess through the Holy Spirit living in you. Fear wants to replace your confidence and boldness with doubt and worry so that you lose sight of the covering you have when you're in God's will.

When I was struggling with fear and anxiety, I was led to Psalm 27:1, "The Lord is my light and salvation—so why should I be afraid?" I want to pose the same question to you that I had to ask myself: What has replaced God as your safe place?

What has stepped in and replaced God as your security and protection? When you truly trust God, and allow Him to be your security, fear will cease. When you stop feeding your fears more than you feed the truth of God being who He says He is, you get to a place where you don't break every time things don't work out. You don't care if you face opposition, rejection, or even failure because you know success isn't measured by this world's standard. You eventually get to a place where you can say, "I want to be where God wants me to be. Satan, you can try to keep me from getting there, but I will fight my way through. I will rest in God's truth, who He is, and what His Word says about who I am in Him."

It's difficult to arrive to this place when your fear is rooted in a misrepresentation of how you think God views you. Instead of Him being your safe place where you can be honest and vulnerable, you sit back in condemnation and say, "I don't feel safe being in this intimate space with You to tell You the deepest things in my heart; I'm afraid You might reject me. I'm afraid You might not receive it. You might be disappointed in me because that's how someone else responded when I tried to be open and honest with them."

The devil is a liar and a snatcher of edges. In other words, nothing good can come from entertaining his shenanigans. Stop believing the lies he tries to feed you!

God is not like people! A lot of times we're walking around with a spirit of fear because we're so afraid to fail God, but He wants you to see that where He's calling you to is a safe place. He will protect you there.

Now hear me out; God will call you to some places that are uncomfortable. Trust me, I haven't seen my comfort zone since 2010. God will take you out of familiar territory, require you to mature, and He will prune you of things that don't look like Him. But He covers you in that place.

I know you might be afraid because it's new, it's different, or it requires you to change, but it's safe for you to follow God into the unknown. He's not going to lead you somewhere that He doesn't go and He's not going to abandon you when you get there. When you stay in a place that God hasn't told you to be, you risk being uncovered; that's more unsafe than being uncomfortable.

If what God is requiring of you takes you out of your comfortable place, will you still give Him a yes? Are you willing to be where He is even if it requires a sacrifice on your behalf that is greater than anything that has been required of you before? If where God is leading you pushes you so far out of your comfort zone that you have no control and you have no choice but to cling tightly to Him, are you willing to go there? If where He is requires you to quit the job, break off the friendship, leave the relationship, or pack up and leave your family, will you trust Him and obey?

It's easy to sing the songs about surrender; it's easy to sing about wanting to be where He is. What happens when it becomes more than a song and He requires you to make difficult decisions? Will you obey Him or will you allow fear to stagnate you from walking in your God-ordained purpose? Trust and believe wherever it is that He is leading you, there's purpose and He will meet you there.

Psalm 56:3 reminds us that when we are afraid, we should put our trust in Him. If fear is keeping you from pursuing the things that God has promised or spoken over your life, ask yourself what you have put your trust in. Is it in your patterns with disappointment and letdowns instead of trusting that God has created a path and gone before you? Are you trusting the opinions and recommendations of others who say, "not right now, that doesn't make sense," or "why would you do that?" Are you more reliant on the labels that people have attached to you that say you aren't good enough than to what God says about you?

Sometimes our fear that God won't be able to take care of us or our problems is greater than the truth and belief that He can. Allow God to be your peace in the midst of fear. Stop worrying about what tomorrow is going to bring and fearing things that may never even happen. The enemy knows your fears and insecurities just as God does and Satan loves to fuel the fire of your up-and-down emotions.

It's time to put that fire out.

Do you know what happens when you stop feeding something? It will eventually starve. Stop feeding those thoughts that you know are not of God. The fact that He has not given us a spirit of fear was not a fun tidbit added to the Bible for kicks and giggles. It was put there because it is the true Word of the living God. I don't know what you believe, but I still believe God to be the Great I Am and not "the great I might be," or the "great I was." Take your focus off fear and allow God to establish your foundation on truth—and not your fickle emotions. I believe that God has placed amazing gifts and talents on the inside of you, and I pray you won't allow fear to hinder them from coming forth.

Chapter 5
Forgiveness
I Forgive You, Kind of, Sort of...Not Really

➤➤➤➤➤➤➤ ⸺⸺⸺ ⸻⸻⸻

This week I had a crash course in practicing what I preach. I received a call where I was informed that someone had relayed information about me that wasn't quite accurate. It felt like an attempt to throw me under the bus, so needless to say, I had to have a come-to-Jesus moment to get my thoughts together. Just as things were calming down, there were multiple pop quizzes thrown into the mix, just to add a little fun to the, "how can we test Angel's entire life?" party.

My initial thoughts regarding all of this were not warm and fuzzy. I wanted to be upset and focus on what was said or done, and I even wanted to complain to others about it. Each time, I felt a tug when I arrived at the crossroad of choosing to harden my heart or to forgive and keep it moving. After every test, I always had a sense of the Holy Spirit saying, "Let it go." Did I want to? No; but I've been down that road before, and I've learned that the weight of holding grudges and refusing to forgive is far too heavy for me to bear.

When we're struggling with forgiveness, we easily justify our reasoning to not forgive a person. Just as people tend to categorize levels of sin, we also like to determine what is forgivable based on our level of offense. Jesus, however, told the disciples to forgive those who sin against them (Matthew 6:14). He doesn't follow this sentence up with, "Forgive them only if they didn't do x, y, or z." Instead, Jesus tells them, "If you refuse to forgive others, your Father will not forgive your sins" (Matthew 6:15).

Harsh reality, right?

Our refusal to forgive has an impact on God forgiving us, but we don't tend to look at it in that way when we are the offended. We'll cry out to God and roll around on the floor, right before folding into the fetal position when we need forgiveness and grace. But when someone does something to wrong us, we will carry that grudge for years all while maintaining a smile and perfect composure in their presence.

I've been one of those people. I've rocked many grudges as a part of my attire. I didn't even realize how it was a weight that I was dragging alongside me. I've struggled with forgiveness for a very large part of my life and I still have to check my heart in this area. Several friendships have suffered because of the grudges I have held on to. A hardened heart became my defense mechanism to avoid having difficult conversations that would leave me vulnerable and require me to deal with my hurt. I've chosen to cut people off without explanation instead of dealing with issues, forgiving them, and moving forward. I've found comfort in avoiding conflict by shutting down and dismissing people from my life as I convinced myself that it was better than potentially being hurt by them again.

This mindset proved to be destructive and quite unfulfilling. I found myself alone and burdened down with anger, resentment, bitterness, and a *woe is me* mentality. I learned that just because I refused to deal with things, it didn't make them magically disappear. In contrast, the hurt and wounds that I refused to deal with eventually started dealing with me.

The truth is, forgiveness can be difficult sometimes. It requires you to be vulnerable and it's never a one-time choice to forgive. The realization that it's something you must *choose* to do is daunting in itself. It's always easier to say you forgive someone than to choose to walk in forgiveness. Sometimes it is a daily choice to cast down negative thoughts towards that person and to shut down your mind's attempts to rehash what they did wrong. In addition to this, forgiveness requires a level of discernment with people and also with yourself. When dealing with offenses, it's important to examine your heart just as you're looking at the intent of others.

Although it may be a hard truth to accept, we must learn that how we perceive things are not always the reality of what they are or how they happened. In other words, it's not always everyone else who is wrong; sometimes it's you.

I've had to learn to take all matters to God before I bring a problem to a person because sometimes it's not even an issue. There were times where I was simply being too sensitive and I made something bigger than it truly was. When you take your issues and cares to God, it puts you in an environment that can break down the hard shells around your heart that hold on to offense. It allows you to step back from feelings and examine what transpired from a rational mindset versus an emotional place. I don't know about you, but I'd rather have those messy emotional conversations with God before I have it with a person.

Another reason why discernment is important is that although it is necessary to forgive, it's not always necessary to continue a relationship with people. It's very easy to mistake forgiveness with reconciliation when they don't necessarily go hand-in-hand. It might not be God's plan for a person to continue in your life, but it is His will for you to be free from the bondage of being unforgiving.

I'm grateful God restored some of my friendships, but there were others that were not restored. When I look at the relationships that were restored, I can truly say that they were with people who I knew wanted God's best for me. Even our conflict revealed issues within myself that I needed to deal with to become a better person and to look more like Christ. Although they were challenging, those relationships and incidents also showed me valuable lessons in handling conflict.

I learned the importance of communicating and forgiving quickly. The longer you go without addressing an issue, the more time convinces you that it's not worth repairing. When you have problems that you allow to linger, it tends to manifest a lot of feelings under the surface that typically go unacknowledged. In return, anger, resentment, hurt, sadness, etc., start to show up in passive aggressive ways until you eventually hit your breaking point. When it gets to that point, it's typically just a big mess. It appears as if it came from nowhere when it had actually been brewing for quite some time.

From the relationships that weren't restored, I learned that forgiveness does not require a person to be sorry. When you choose to forgive a person who never apologized or attempted to make things right, you then experience freedom from the attachment of their wrong. Sometimes people won't get it. They won't see their fault or acknowledge that they've wronged or hurt you. Forgive them anyway. Choosing not to only becomes a hindrance to you.

When you find yourself replaying the wrong or wanting to be upset with them, pray for them. I don't mean a prayer like, "The Bible says, 'Touch not My anointed and do My prophet no harm,' so I rebuke sister spandex in Jesus Name" (Psalm 105:15). Nah, baby that's still rooted in hurt. Genuinely pray for them and ask God to work in their heart and extend His grace and mercy to them.

It's so important to release the burden of not forgiving others, and it's equally important to deal with the underlying factors of this struggle. If you find yourself constantly struggling with forgiveness, it's time to identify the root. For some people, the reason they have a hard time with this is because they are dealing with a spirit of offense. A person dealing with a spirit of offense is usually easily triggered. This type of spirit convinces them that people are always attempting to wrong them. They often perceive that they are treated unfairly when things don't work out. They usually have a difficult time receiving correction because they feel that they're being slighted or attacked.

When you are trying to break free from the spirit of offense, you must learn how to not take things personally. I know that's so much easier said than done, but just hear me out! In Matthew 18:21, we learn that Peter asked Jesus, "Lord, how often should I forgive someone who sins against me? Seven times?" Now we can talk later about how brother Pete thought he was impressing Jesus by saying seven times, but for now, I want to focus on a keyword in his question. He asked how often he should forgive someone who sinned against *him*.

Did you catch it?

When you're dealing with a spirit of offense, you tend to take things as a personal attack. Understand that as a child of God, when people mistreat you, hurt you, and talk about you, the true sin is against God.

Let's look at David for example; in Psalm 51:4, David prayed and told God, "Against You, and You alone have I sinned." Just in case you don't know what the sin was that he was referring to, let me give you a little background. Although David is known as the man after

God's own heart and the author of some of our favorite scriptures in Psalm, he had some issues (Acts 13:22). He committed adultery with Bathsheba, got her pregnant, and then had her husband murdered (2 Samuel 11:1-27). I don't know about you, but I could imagine Bathsheba's husband, Uriah, probably would have felt some type of way if he were alive to hear David's prayer. He would've probably said, "Man, what do you mean you only sinned against God? You got me *all the way* messed up, David!"

It seems like this could be one of those instances that could be deemed as justifiable to refuse to forgive, right? Could we really fault Uriah if he didn't want to forgive David? Truth be told, that's how we often feel when someone does something wrong to us. We measure their indiscretion by hurt and offense and then we look for others to validate how we feel. Know that when people sin, it has the ability to hurt other people. Does that make it right or okay? Absolutely not, but the ultimate offense is against God.

God will deal with the person who wronged you, but you must release the offense to him. Surrender the hurt, pain, and frustration to the Lord and allow Him to take that burden off of you and trust Him with it. As you give it to God and forgive the person, it's not then about waiting for God to "get them." Yes, we know that God dealt with David's sins and there were consequences for his actions, but He also still restored David after he repented (2 Samuel 12:13-24). If we solely forgive with the mindset of wanting God to gut-punch people with His wrath, we've completely missed the point of forgiveness.

When working through forgiveness, it's important to acknowledge that when someone wrongs you, you don't have any control over that. You can't control what people do or say, but you do have control over whether you choose to be offended. The spirit of offense wants you to hold on to wrongs. It wants you to hold grudges so that bitterness and frustration will take root in your heart. It can even mask your pride as it emphasizes the wrong and validates your emotions that encourage you to not forgive.

Pride convinces people that it's weak to forgive someone who hurt them. They feel like their offender doesn't deserve their forgiveness. The prideful have an inner struggle because they believe that if they forgive, then they are giving that person the power. Forgiving a person does not mean that what they did was right or that you even understand why they did it. It does, however, set you free from the weight and burden of carrying the offense around. It's important to forgive; otherwise, you just continue to carry around a record of wrongs for everyone who has offended you. Trust me, you don't have time for that!

When Peter asked Jesus how many times they should forgive, Jesus told him "until seventy times seven" (Matthew 18:22, KJV). Just in case your anointing isn't in math, that is 490 times. The purpose behind Jesus saying this is not to set a limit on how many times we should forgive, but instead to affirm that we shouldn't keep a record of wrongs. If anyone has time to make a checklist and tell someone, "Alright you're at 394 times that I've forgiven you; you're about to run out," then we've got a bigger problem on our hands. No judgment here; I'm just saying there's a special kind of altar call for that person.

The point is that we should continue to forgive because God continues to forgive us. When we don't allow God to soften our heart for forgiveness to take place, we fail to see the trap that Satan has set before us. As believers, we need to be aware of the bait that the enemy dangles to distract us. We know that he comes to kill, steal, and destroy, but we're often oblivious to the tactics he uses to do this in our own lives (John 10:10).

Satan is messy. He likes to set traps that operate in confusion. The trap that he sets against forgiveness is destruction and division, and the bait that he uses is offense. He uses that as the bait because he realizes if he can keep you focused on the offense, then it will harden your heart towards forgiveness. This will eventually draw a wedge between you and other people which will lead to division. You should recognize the trap because it is the very tactic that he is using to divide marriages, families, and churches.

The enemy knows the significance and power that comes from unity and people getting on one accord, so he desires to cause division. He recognizes that division distracts from *the vision*. It shifts your focus from the purpose that God has for your life and the people connected to you, to their wrongs. Satan plays on this by setting little traps to stir up conflict. He sets traps with an offense here and there that he knows you will keep a record of for a rainy day.

You might not be able to remember where you parked your car at Walmart, but you can quote verbatim what someone said that upset you on January 23, 2013, at 9:43 p.m. eastern standard time.

I can't tell you how many times I have pulled information from archive files during a disagreement. I'm talking about stuff that I swore I had forgiven the person for and moved on from. Better yet, I can recall even more times when I was upset with someone who had no clue why I was mad, and it wasn't because they were too oblivious to know. I was simply upset over something that I never even told them I was mad about.

There are so many people who are upset with their spouse, boyfriend, family member, best friend, and whoever else because they were offended by something that the person doesn't even know about. My pastor always talks to me about the importance of letting people know what my expectations are. He has always told me that I can't be upset with someone for not meeting expectations that I never articulated. In other words, people are not mind-readers, so don't assume that a person knows what you want or what you're thinking if you didn't say it.

Understand that the breeding ground for offense in any relationship is bad communication.

People are walking around with hardened hearts thinking that a person should *know* that they're upset without them saying it. Listen, it might be common sense to you, but common sense is not as common in these streets as one would like for it to be. If you have an issue, talk to the person about it before you get in your feelings and catch an attitude over something that you assume they should know. It's all a part of the trap. Until you recognize this, you're never going to realize how the little stuff can become big issues that divide and destroy your relationships. Instead of focusing on their wrong, shift your focus to the grace that is extended to you by the Lord, and extend that same grace to others.

I had to give myself this reminder when I was faced with a situation where I felt led to reach out to someone to make peace with them. If I can be honest, my initial reaction was very immature. I questioned why I had to be the one to make it right when I wasn't the one who did anything wrong. God humbled me so quickly with the thought of Jesus going to Him and asking the same question: "Why do I have to die for the sins of these people who don't even want to obey You? I have never sinned, yet I have to go make it right for them."

Okay, God, I repent.

I'm going to go ahead and make this phone call right quick. My bad...

How easy is it to want God to extend His grace to us while we refuse to extend it to others? I'm reminded of the parable of the debtor whose debts were forgiven but when he was in the exact same position to forgive someone else's debt, he handled the man ruthlessly and threw him in prison (Matthew 18:23-35). How dare we think that we're deserving of forgiveness while we choose to withhold it from others?

You might be thinking, "But Angel, you don't know what they did to me!" You're right, and I'm not attempting to minimize it or say that it doesn't matter. I do suggest looking at Jesus as an example though. As He is hanging on the cross, He says, "Father forgive them; for they know not what they do" (Luke 23:34, KJV). Mind you, He is being crucified even though He is blameless. He's laying down His life for all mankind—including those who put Him on the cross. The people who mocked, beat, ridiculed, and attempted to make Him out to be a liar, were the same people He asked God to forgive.

I want to encourage you to release whatever it is that is hindering you from forgiveness. There's a beautiful exchange that happens within the release. As you cast your cares on the Lord, a burden is released from you in exchange for rest, freedom, peace, and restoration. I truly believe that God desires to release some things to His people, but we also must release some things to make room to receive what He has for us. Ask God to soften your heart and heal you from within. Leave it with Him. Whatever it is, forgive. Let God have it.

Chapter 6
Avoidance
I Don't Want to Talk About It

-»»»»»————————«««««-

"Hi, I'm Angel—crowd says, "Hi, Angel"— "and I am a foodie."

I know I'm shaped like a lean piece of chocolate asparagus, but believe me when I say that food has a special place in my heart. I love food almost as much as I love my momma. No, seriously, it's a pretty close second. I love to eat. Like, all the time. I eat even when I'm not hungry. Chewing is some type of comforting mechanism that reaches all the way down to my big toe. I don't think you can fully understand how food is my love language and how it brings joy to my soul.

I even find myself doing a little happy dance almost every time I eat. I'm talking a full-on side-to-side shuffle and a pitter patter of my feet under the table. If it's extra amazing, I just might jump back into the 90s and raise the roof for 2.3 seconds. If it were socially acceptable, I'd probably eat all day.

People are generally surprised to see how much I eat. When you look at my size in comparison to my lack of portion control, it doesn't quite match. I'll admit that I've taken advantage of a graciously high metabolism that has made it hard for me to gain or keep on weight. I'm aware that this is a horrible excuse to indulge in Wendy's four-for-four dollars deal, but what can I say?

Side note, whoever came up with that idea for Wendy's deserves a raise and the promise that their hairline will never thin. Just saying...

Back to the point at hand, I love food! Partially because it tastes good, but also because I'm a bit of an emotional eater. Yes, I am one of those people who likes to eat their feelings away. Food has helped me to avoid so many different things that I didn't even recognize how I had used it as a crutch for years. Whenever I find myself feeling overwhelmed, stressed out, or in a funk, I typically turn to food. It's almost like my emotions crave the greasiest of burgers, fried anything, and the sweetest dessert to appease their frustrations.

I also find myself using food to my advantage to help my introvert struggle. Although I am an introvert at heart, I'm sometimes forced to be an extrovert because ministry has required me to be more sociable and outgoing. My social awkwardness, however, becomes obvious when I have to make small talk with people.

Can I just bring you into my socially-stressed mind for two minutes? Whenever I have a lunch or dinner date with someone who I don't know or don't know well, I have anxiety about it. I think about how I don't really have to worry about awkward moments of silence when we first sit down, because we'll be looking at the menu to figure out what we're going to eat. Once the menus are gone, that becomes a game-changer because we now must talk to each other. I know there are people who can have organic conversations about anything; I am not one of those people. I need to have talking points in mind, otherwise, I'm going to draw a blank and just sit there quietly. I'm perfectly okay with silence, but I realize it tends to make other people uncomfortable, so I try not to be *awkward Angel.*

By the time our orders have been placed, I have at least three talking points in my head and I'm hoping that the other person will say enough to carry a conversation that will last until our food comes. As they're talking, I'm listening intently, not because I'm such a great listener, but because I'm trying to find something to respond with that connects with what they're talking about. Once the food comes, I'm in there like swimwear because if I can't think of anything to say, I just keep putting food in my mouth. It's rude to talk with your mouth full, right? Right.

Welcome to my brain.

Yes, it's quite exhausting, but food comes in the clutch and helps your girl out.

Now you may be thinking "Angel, honey, girlfriend, boo thang, step away from the table." You might have even raised an eyebrow at my shenanigans. That's okay, but take a moment to ask yourself, "What is *my* vice?" It can be anything that you turn to, to escape from dealing with what you need to. It might not be food, but we all have something we turn to or have turned to, that quiets the ache of our frustration, discouragement, or discontentment and it's not always God.

The Holy Spirit had to check me on this. God revealed to me that I was using food as a coping mechanism to avoid facing my issues. I used to also do this with shopping because, come on, who doesn't love a little retail therapy? Whenever I would have a hard day at work or was just in a mood, I'd buy new clothes, shoes, or makeup. There's just something about having new stuff that appears to give you a nice little energy boost. The Lord eventually checked me on that as well, and I didn't even recognize how I had substituted one struggle with another while I continued to avoid my problems.

It's easy to do that as you look for something, anything really, to distract you from facing what you need to. Some people turn to alcohol, drugs, cigarettes, sex, or people. For others, they become so consumed by activity that they're too busy to have to think about their problems. They're overly-involved in church, a workaholic, or a part of tons of groups or organizations. If they have something to do or think about, it distracts them from getting quiet enough to deal with what is revealed in the silence.

The issue with all of this is that regardless of what you choose to turn to, they're all temporary fixes outside of God. They will only stall, not erase, the inevitable— dealing with your issues. It was easier for me to eat my feelings because I preferred stifling them instead of dealing with them. It gave me the temporary fix that I was looking for and it wasn't accompanied by tears or further frustration that I desired to avoid. I just stuffed my issues on the shelf of my heart until there was no more room for them.

Then *bam!*

Everything that was stuffed began to unravel all at once and it brought along its friends, sister overwhelmed and brother irritated. What I had stuffed and dismissed came oozing out in ways that I could no longer avoid. The weight of that was beyond what I could continue to manage. We often fail to realize that avoiding issues, thoughts, and feelings don't just make them disappear. They will start dealing with you in your household, at your job, in school, and most importantly, in your mind. But you'll continue to put off doing or saying whatever it is that you need to because it appears that it's easier to dismiss it than to face it.

Why is that so? What is it that you're avoiding and what is hindering you from dealing with it? Is it fear, doubt, worry, anger, frustration, or uncertainty? Identify your *why* because that is what reveals your *what*. *Why* you're avoiding will help you to deal with *what* you're avoiding. Avoidance is just the surface-level issue, but there's a source that is feeding your reaction to avoid. Until you identify the source, you'll waste time treating a symptom but never the actual problem. Some people are okay with that, because the source is what they're usually avoiding.

The irony in this is, as women, we're natural problem solvers. We will put so much effort and energy into finding a solution and making sure that everyone else is okay. We'll take on the responsibility of taking care of everything and everyone as we take care of ourselves last, if at all. We'll appear to be superwoman, but deep down we're tired. Not just any kind of tired either; our soul is tired. We're drained, empty, and trying to manage on yesterday's strength, that's fragile at best. In our roles of being a mother, wife, pastor's wife, sister, daughter, and/or friend, we can sometimes lose sight of just being *us*. We're so used to being something to someone else that we don't always get to be something to, or for, ourselves. This is not because we forget or don't want to, but sometimes it may feel like we don't get the opportunity to. It's amazing how we even avoid thinking about this, because there's a sense of guilt almost of feeling this way.

You don't want to acknowledge that you're tired, frustrated, overwhelmed, overworked, and stressed. You don't want to admit that the thought popped in your mind that the kids who you prayed for get on your nerves at times. You still love them, but sometimes they try your entire salvation. You don't want to come across bossy because your husband is great, but if you have to repeat what you've already said fifty-eleven times, you just might scream opera-style. You don't want to complain because you prayed for that job and you are grateful to have it, but you also hate it and you wake up every morning questioning, "Do I really *need* this paycheck?"

Can we be real or not?

Avoiding this doesn't make it nonexistent; it just creates a pot on the inside of you that is being slowly stirred with everything that you stuff. God is waiting for you to give it to Him and talk to Him about it, but you keep bringing Him what you think He wants to hear from you. When Peter said, "Give all your worries and cares to God, for he cares about you," he wasn't just referring to the put-together worries that you think are easy to manage (1 Peter 5:7). He meant all of it. You have to realize that God can handle your mess. He can handle your hurts, frustrations, brokenness, bad attitudes, moods swings, and whatever else.

Somewhere along the way, we've been convinced that God only wants the happy and hopeful version of us. Whenever we think or feel something that is wrong, we don't want to address it because it's ugly. So, we unconsciously tell ourselves that we shouldn't or that we can't feel that way. Just because you shouldn't, doesn't mean that you don't. I can't tell you how many times I've had some jacked-up thoughts about things and people. I've had to step back like, "Ooh girl, wait a minute. Let's have a come-to-Jesus moment!" I've started some prayers with, "God, I know this is ugly," or "I know I shouldn't feel this way." But I did. I had to recognize that silencing it would not only affect my attitude, but it would also influence my posture before God.

Instead of just avoiding my issues, I would also start avoiding Him. I would slowly pull away as I would only release what I was willing to give. The once intimate and freeing place of His presence would instead become one of inner conflict as I battled with sharing only what I was willing to face. It wasn't until I decided that I didn't want to pretend with God that I was able to give myself permission to feel. This meant being honest with my frustrations, what I didn't understand, and what was at the core of my heart, even if it was messy. I was able to say, "God, I know this is wrong. I know it's a mess. But I'm giving it to You. I'm giving You my truth."

I want you to give yourself permission to feel. Notice I didn't say to be led by how you feel, but to simply *feel*. Don't dismiss it and don't start doing other stuff to keep your mind off it. Too often, we feel like we're supposed to appear to be put-together, happy, and positive, even when we are not. If we cry, then we're weak and emotional. If we speak our truth, then we're complaining and ungrateful. So, we suck it up, suck it in, and respond with "I'm fine" as we struggle with hoping that no one sees that we are not, while also desperately wanting someone to care enough to recognize that "fine" is just a rehearsed line.

Let's discuss a woman who knew God and loved Him, but found herself in a place that rocked her to her core. This is a woman who spoke openly about how she felt given her circumstances. Her name was Naomi. When we read Ruth 1:20, Naomi states that the Lord made her life very bitter. She even goes as far as telling the women in

Bethlehem to call her Mara, which translates to bitter. Now before you roll your eyes at her, let me give you some context.

Naomi had her family uprooted from Israel after a severe famine hit the land (Ruth 1:1). Once they settled in Moab, her husband died. Then, ten years later, both her sons died (Ruth 1:3-4). She's left widowed and childless with no one around her except her two daughters in law, Ruth and Orpah. The Levirate marriage law stated that if a woman was widowed, it was expected that the next kin of the deceased husband was to marry the widow to carry on the family legacy (Deuteronomy 25:5-6). Naomi had no other family in Moab, so she returned to Israel with Ruth. She returned to the place that she left due to a famine, feeling even more barren.

When she arrived, she said, "I went away full, but the Lord has brought me home empty. Why call me Naomi when the Lord has caused me to suffer and the Almighty has sent such tragedy upon me?" (Ruth 1:20-21).

That's heavy, but it's honest.

Put yourself in her shoes for a moment. I could imagine her thinking about how she's returning to a place worse off then when she left it. The place that was already associated with loss, emptiness, and sadness now serves as another reminder that she's experienced even greater loss since she left. She's bitter. That's her truth.

Maybe it's not difficult for you to put yourself in her shoes because this, too, is your truth. It might not be the exact same situation, but maybe you came out of a season where you felt stripped. You experienced a loss, whether it was a job, relationship, or finances, and you came out of that season feeling empty and dry. You thought that as you transitioned to the new job, the new church, the new city, the new house, it would be different. Yet you find yourself in a situation again where you feel like you're still losing.

Perhaps you had to return to a place that you thought you never would have returned to. You had to go back to a 9-5 after you tried to start your own business. You had to move back home because things didn't go as planned. You found yourself back in the same type of relationship that failed before. You find yourself, just like Naomi, feeling empty and questioning why life has dealt you this hand.

God, why is this my portion?

Do You not see?

Do You not care?

Why do I have to go through this?

Can I get a break for once?

Can You help a sista out?!

What do you do when the weight of what you're carrying feels like it's too much and you don't understand why God hasn't intervened yet? You know that His Word says that He has a plan for your life, but this plan appears to be filled with pain, emptiness, and disappointment.

We've gotten so used to putting on face and pretending to be content when we're going through it that we ignore the fact that we're frustrated with God. The truth is, sometimes we avoid bringing our issues to Him because our issue *is* Him. Yikes! We don't want to acknowledge that we don't understand why He allowed certain things to happen while others don't. We don't want to admit that we're frustrated, or dare I say upset, with what He has taken out of our lives, even when it was for our good. We don't want to deal with the reality that we may be a little, or even very, bitter towards God.

I think it's safe to say that this is likely how Naomi felt. She didn't sugarcoat it, either. She didn't try to pretend to be happy or avoid her reality. After she states her frustration, you don't see that she was rebuked or told that she shouldn't feel that way. Could it be that it wasn't that God was ignoring or not concerned with what was going on with her, but that He had already determined that through her bitterness, she would eventually be blessed? While she was focused on the fact that she was bitter, God had already established a plan to restore her.

When Ruth married Boaz and they birthed their son Obed, the women in the town said to Naomi:

Praise the Lord, who has now provided a redeemer for your family! May this child be famous in Israel. May he restore your youth and care for you in your old age. For he is the son of your daughter-in-law who loves you and has been better to you than seven sons (Ruth 4:14-15).

I love that what started off as a story of bitterness, death, and calamity ends in joy, life, and restoration.

Even more so, I love that we see that God met Naomi in her place of honesty. We also see that in her honesty and amid sorrow, she didn't unravel in it. She acknowledged that she was bitter but she didn't allow bitterness to become her new residence. She didn't avoid her reality or her truth. Instead, she owned it and by the end, you see two women, Naomi and Ruth, who trusted God and endured.

I want to remind you that the same God who did it for Naomi will also meet you in your honesty. As life happens, it can be easy to forget that before you had any type of role or title, you were His daughter. You *still* are His daughter and He cares about every single detail of your life. He knows that you don't understand. He knows that you question *why* and *when*. He wants you to know that He sees you. He's for you. He's with you always. He hasn't left you and He hasn't forsaken you. He knows this season seems so dry and empty and you've thought about giving up more than you have desired to press forward. He knows that you've tried to drown the hurt, pain, depression, suicidal thoughts, and anxiety in so many things. You've tried to avoid facing what is before you, and as it presents itself it feels like life is snatching the rug from under your feet.

He knows. Gosh, He knows. He wants you to stop running. He *needs* you to stop running. He wants you to know that He understands that because you're used to having to be strong for everyone else that you feel as though you can't break. You can't cry, you can't fall apart, and you can't be broken.

You *can*, and it's okay.

You need to know that it's okay not to be okay. When you bring frustrations to God, He will receive them and He will restore you. He doesn't need you to be superwoman. He doesn't need you to be perfectly polished and presentable. He wants you as you are—broken bitter, frustrated, angry, and whatever else.

He will meet you there.

He will love you there.

He will heal you there.

He will make you whole there.

The Lord hears his people when they call to him for help. He rescues them from all their troubles. The Lord is close to the brokenhearted; he rescues those whose spirits are crushed (Psalm 34:17-18).

Chapter 7
Settling
But He's Fine, Though

➤➤➤➤➤➤ ───────── ⟨⟨⟨⟨⟨⟨⟨

I had a dream one night that I was at my wedding. I watched the whole thing play out as if it were a movie.

The wedding took place in a spacious backyard of a gorgeous mansion. The flowers were crisp white, the décor had accents of gold, and everything looked stunning. It was picture-perfect. I couldn't have asked for a more beautiful wedding. Oh, and did I mention my husband was foine? Yes, so fine I had to add an "o" for emphasis!

As I looked around, I realized that out of all the faces that were present, none of them were familiar to me. I looked at my bridesmaids and thought, "seriously, who are these people?" As I was watching, I found it odd that none of my best friends were a part of my wedding party. My parents weren't present and no one from my church attended my wedding. It was only the grooms' friends and family who were there. I could tell in the movie that I was not surprised by this, but I definitely was watching it as a viewer.

The wedding took place, the pictures were posted, and we lived happily ever after.

Yeah, not quite.

After the wedding, the movie skipped to a few weeks later and my husband had not been home! Well, let me rephrase. He would come home for a couple of hours, but then he would leave and be gone for the rest of the day and night. Needless to say, this was not what I signed up for. I sat on our bed thinking, "What is going on?" We were newlyweds, so we should've been enjoying our new union and spending time with one another. That wasn't happening.

In the next scene, I walk through the mall and I pull out my phone to text two of my best friends. I type their names into a group message and then I put my phone away. I would pull it back out and stare at it for a moment, only to type a sentence and then delete it. My hesitation revealed that there had been quite some time since we last spoke. I eventually sent them a message explaining what was going on. I told them I didn't know what to do about my marriage and I didn't understand what was going on with my husband.

They never responded to me.

I could see that I was disappointed in the movie, but it also appeared that I understood their lack of response. At this point, I was discouraged because I didn't have any friends or family to reach out to. I felt all alone.

Fast forward a few more scenes. My husband is home more, but every time he's home, there are always random men coming to the house. I could sense the shadiness that was taking place from a mile away. They were doing handshakes where it was clear that something was being passed from person to person. As I'm watching, I said, "Angel, we messed around and married a drug dealer girl!" Like the one who is in charge type of drug dealer. I'm sitting on the bed with tears in my eyes as I think, "What have I gotten myself into?"

Then I woke up.

I immediately questioned if I ate pork before I went to sleep as I thought about how bizarre my dream was. As I started to think about it more, the Lord began to show me that a lot of times, we get so caught up on wanting the perfect relationship or wedding, that we end up settling to get it. We'll get consumed by the idea of wanting to be with someone, having the perfect wedding, or getting married so that we can finally have sex—let's be honest—and we ignore all the red flags that we settled for.

We end up putting ourselves in a position where we settle for someone who we are not supposed to be with just for the sake of having someone around. Then we get frustrated when God gives us a clear *no* about a person in our life because we've waited this long for a relationship and we don't want to give it up. We do what we want and we end up in a relationship or marriage that's unfulfilling because we were more worried about the wedding than the covenant.

I had a beautiful wedding. It looked like something you would see on TV. That's how extravagant it was. But my marriage was trash. I was unhappy and I had yoked myself up with someone who ended up being a burden to me. The reason why none of my friends or family were there was because none of them supported me marrying that person. They saw what I refused to see. They had tried to warn me about him, but I chose to ignore it.

It's true that not every person needs to be in your relationship, but you need to have accountability and people who can be honest with you about things that you may overlook. Everyone isn't hating on your relationship or trying to keep you from the altar. Take heed to the people who are pointing out the red flags that you don't see. Of course, you can pray, fast, and seek the Holy Spirit to confirm what someone is saying, but also recognize that people are not trying to break up what you think is your happily-ever-after. Sometimes God is using them to warn you about He is trying to protect you from.

When you're in love or lust, there will be issues that you don't acknowledge about your significant other simply because you don't want to. You don't want to see the wrong, so you dismiss it. You'll accept and tolerate different behavior, knowing that you deserve better, but you don't want to have to start over with someone new. You'll settle because he's *good enough* and it's better than having to spend another year alone. Then you'll start justifying why it's okay for you to be with him based off what he *doesn't* do.

He might not be the best mate, but at least he doesn't cheat on me.

At least he doesn't hit me.

At least he doesn't do drugs.

Why are we giving out gold stickers to men who aren't doing things that they shouldn't be doing, anyway? It's great that he doesn't do those things, but that should be the expectation, not a bonus. A bonus is if the man can cook, not that he doesn't throw stuff upside your head.

The danger with settling is that it leads you to disregard offenses as you accept different actions all while hoping that it will eventually change. You look at that person's potential and think about what they *could* become, but you don't take the time to consider how they also have the potential to never reach that point. There's nothing wrong with believing in what a person could be, but you also need to take at face value who they currently are. If a man shows you that the only fruit he produces are oranges, and you know you hate oranges, don't be mad at him if you marry him and he continues to produce oranges and not grapes like you hoped he would. He showed you who he was, but you chose to see what you thought he could be instead. The fruit isn't going to change simply because vows were exchanged.

These are things to consider before your relationship even progresses to the point of a proposal, let alone a wedding. But to do this, you must acknowledge if you're settling and if so, why are you willing to do so?

As women, we're often pressured to settle down, get married, and have children as we're reminded that our ovaries won't always be a spring chicken. When I was twenty-five, someone asked me, "Angel, how does it feel to be your age, not married, and without children?" My response was, "It feels like I trust God to prepare me for that part of my life when He's ready." That was four years ago and the thought of her asking me that still irritates me. This wasn't even someone who knew me that well! I wanted to suggest that she go play in traffic while holding sharp objects, but Jesus helped me to guard my tongue.

I wish that was the only time I got asked that question. The closer I've gotten to thirty, however, its less of a question and more of me being told what I should be thinking about at this stage of my life. This is usually equated to being a wife and/or mother in my near future. I can only imagine that the pressure intensifies as thirty becomes thirty-five, then forty, then fifty, and so on. You get tired of waiting or you've invested too much time with someone to leave and rebuild with someone else. You feel like time isn't on your side so it's better to take what's available than to wait for someone who you don't even know exists.

You'll start doing the math in your head of how if you leave your current situation, it might be a year or more before you meet someone else. Then you'll date that person for a year or more before you get engaged. Now you have a couple of months to a year or more before you get married, and you want to enjoy your first year or two of marriage without kids. So, you're looking at maybe five years before you have children, but you're already thirty-five now and it wasn't your plan to have kids in your forties. You look at your current option, and although it's not what you want, it's convenient because you already have it.

It might seem like that's *doing the most*, but those are real thoughts and fears that some women have. They settle not necessarily because they want to, but because they feel like it's their only option.

We have to guard our hearts and mind against people who, intentionally or otherwise, try to pressure us to get to where they think we should be. Our timeline has to be based on God's timing and not the rushed timing of people. The funny thing about people is that they will rush you into getting married and having babies, but when it falls apart or when you need help, those same people will likely be MIA. Don't allow people to guilt you into feeling like you should get married by a certain time so that you can have a gut full of human before your biological clock breaks and your eggs scramble. Don't allow their words, wedding pictures on Facebook, or anything else to cause you to settle or doubt God's timing for your life.

Being single for the last nine years, I can understand the desire to want to be in a relationship and eventually get married; especially as you see beautiful couples who are in love with their spouse and who did it God's way. You look on with your heart screaming, "I want that!" Trust me, I get it! But as women who really want to grow in Christ, we can't afford to settle. You become one with the person who you marry (Mark 10:8). Their issues now become your issues and guess what—everyone has issues! Even that great, fine, Christian man you've been praying for will have some issues, so you can imagine what kind of problems Lucifer Jr. who you settle for will have.

The person who you choose to join yourself with will have a significant impact on your life. Ephesians 5:23 tells us that the husband is the head of the wife, so therefore, that man is responsible for leading you. If you desire to have children, he's also responsible for leading his family towards Christ. He will have a direct impact on your relationship with God as well as your children's relationship with God. The nature of that impact and his leadership is going to be determined by his own relationship with God.

Understand that even if he doesn't have a relationship with God, that doesn't mean that he doesn't have the ability to lead. He may even be a great leader, to be honest. Men are natural-born leaders; their instinct is to lead and to take charge. They have innate leadership skills, even when they don't act like a leader. It's important to acknowledge this because a man can be leading you, but it doesn't mean he's leading you to Christ. He may have the ability to lead, but if he doesn't have a relationship with God, the question becomes where, what, and to whom is he leading you to?

This is the reason Apostle Paul says, "Don't team up with those who are unbelievers" (2 Corinthians 6:14);

He's telling us to not put ourselves in a position that could lead us to compromise our faith. As we continue to read this verse, he asked, "How can righteousness be a partner with wickedness? How can light live with darkness?" It's difficult for the two to coincide because one or the other will eventually take over. You might think you can change that person or lead them to Christ, but don't allow pride to lead you to think that they can't also pull you away from Him. These are things to think about before you say I do so you don't end up saying, "Lord, I wish I didn't."

But maybe he's sweet as pie and he has some issues, but he goes to church on occasion and he can quote scripture. Okay, that's cute; so did Satan when he was tempting Jesus in the wilderness (Matthew 4:1-11). Going to church doesn't make a person a believer any more than barking like a dog makes them a Rottweiler. Some of the most disobedient people attend church, sing in the choir, and even preach behind the pulpit. Verbal proclamation of scripture without life application is void. Matthew 7:16 tells us that we can identify a person by their fruit, "that is by the way they act." A man's actions, not just what comes out of his mouth, will tell you who he serves and what he is about. Does he try to honor your purity? What does his prayer life look like? Does he have to go to the table of contents to find out where Genesis is? No shade, but paying attention will give you an idea of his spiritual maturity.

With that being said, you don't just have to be in a relationship where you are unequally yoked to end up settling. We tend to believe that there is a shortage of good Christian men, so if one shows us interest, then we should probably go with him because it's hard to find people really on fire for God. You don't even like him like that, but you'll grow to love him.

Girl, stop.

Leave that man be for who is for him and stop allowing him to simply be a seat filler in your life. Take your focus off your limited thinking that attractive good Christian men are an endangered species. No, ma'am! Jesus could care less about the uneven ratio of men to women in your church, school, or job because limitations have no power over Him. He fed the 5,000 with two fish and five loaves of bread (John 6:1-14). Need I say more?

God knows exactly who He has for you. You can trust Him to get it right. You can also trust that he doesn't need your help. You'll "help" God to find your future boo, only to end up with booboo the fool. God doesn't need you to let Him know that you're ready to be a wife. He is well aware of when it's your time for a spouse.

The problem with singles is that we can tend to feel like we're ready for a mate way before our time because we try to fill a void with a love that only God can fill. We then go out to find our suitable helper instead of allowing God to develop them for us and we end up with a suitable hinderer instead. This person ends up being a headache, but you just *had* to have a man.

Dear friend, rest in God's timing. Seriously, rest. Please, go take a nap.

When we look at the creation of man and woman, it clearly states that it was God who acknowledged that Adam needed a mate (Genesis 2:18). I don't know what all Adam had going on in that garden, but God saw that he needed a suitable helpmeet, which *He* provided when *He* saw the need. Adam was not sulking, coveting, or begging God for a wife. He had not acknowledged that he was lacking anything by not having a spouse.

I know what you're thinking. Go ahead and say it. I'll wait.

"Angel, how could Adam feel like he was lacking something that didn't yet exist? Besides the animals, he was the only human being in the garden! But for us, there are tons of other human beings that make it evident that we're 'missing something' by not having a significant other."

Touché. I hear you. But here's the thing.

Even before Eve was created, Adam was not in the garden by himself; it was him and God. During this time,

Adam did not feel like he was missing out on anything because God was enough. Adam's thoughts were not consumed about wanting a wife or even wanting help because he had God and that was enough for him.

Until you realize that God is enough, you will continue to be consumed in your singleness. You'll feel like you're lacking something and you'll completely miss the beautiful moment of fellowshipping with God when it's just you and Him. You have to learn how to enjoy being in the presence of God without having anyone to distract you. Let's be real, when Eve came into the picture, Adam got a little sidetracked and it led to him disobeying God. Yes, your spouse will be a blessing and should not distract you from God, but marriage does change your relationship with Him. You'll have to learn how to balance your time tending to your family and working on your relationship with the Lord. Apostle Paul even said that it's better for people to remain single because when you're married your focus is divided and you no longer have as much time to devote to the Lord (1 Corinthians 7: 32-35).

Use the time that you have while you're single to be completely focused on the Lord. He knows what you're believing Him for, so don't waste the time that you have in this season being consumed by those desires. Psalm 37:4 tells us to delight ourselves in the Lord and He will give us the desires of our heart. We often focus on the latter half of this scripture while overlooking the part that says to "take delight in the Lord." We make the mistake of putting the focus on the desire when it really should be on God. When we become consumed by our desires instead of Him, we can end up making the desire for a relationship or marriage an idol as we exalt them above Him. Everything that we create an idol out of the devil will indeed use to distract and destruct our relationship with God.

Keep your eyes focused on God and not your left-hand ring finger. The more you focus on being single, the more the enemy will have a field day in your head. He will send you all kinds of fine looking demons, oops I meant men, to get you distracted. Your focus will shift from seeking the kingdom of God, to seeking after a man. You'll talk about wanting this husband more than you'll want to talk with God. Instead of obeying and serving Him out of love and for who He is, you'll end up doing so with the expectation that it will help you to get what you want. Then you convince yourself that if you get serious about following Christ, then that will help to speed up the process of meeting your spouse.

Despite what you may see or think, a spouse is not a reward for living for God—salvation through Jesus Christ is. Your soul not burning in eternal damnation is your reward for serving God, and if He does absolutely nothing else, that is more than enough. If you're serving Him just for what you think He can do for you, then you've missed that He's already done the greatest thing He could ever do.

So, ask yourself: if God tells you that He created you to be single forever, will you still serve Him? Are you done following Him if He doesn't give you what you want? If so, step back and look at your motives for following Christ. We don't serve God to manipulate Him into blessing us or so that we can bargain with him to get a mate. We serve Him because of who He is. It is the least that we can do to thank Him for giving us Jesus to die in our place.

If you recognize that your motives are out of place and that you have made an idol out of relationships, own it. Don't try to twist it to make it pretty or more acceptable for God. He knows your desires, remember. He already knows what you have placed before Him and your intentions in seeking Him. He's aware and He's willing to receive it just as it is. Go before Him with a repentant heart and invite Him in to be your greatest desire above anything and anyone else.

Chapter 8

Sexual Sin

It's Getting Hot in Here

➤➤➤➤➤➤➤——————————————————◀◀◀◀◀◀◀

I wish I could describe the struggle that is happening as I resist the urge to break out in my best rendition of Salt-N-Pepa's song *Let's Talk About Sex*. But can we talk about it? It's such a taboo topic to discuss in general, but especially within the church. It's just assumed that because a person is saved, loves Jesus, attends church, or sings on the worship team that there's absolutely no way they could be struggling with any kind of sexual temptation or sin.

Yeah, that'd be nice if that were the case.

The problem with that mindset is the fact that lust doesn't discriminate. It doesn't care about your title or Christian checklist. All it's concerned about is finding an opened door within your heart and it will take it and run with it. Then you'll find yourself in church, leading, singing, hosting, teaching, preaching, and whatever else, all while you struggle with sexual sin.

But it's never talked about.

You never share it with anyone because you're embarrassed or you're worried about what they might think if they knew what you did when no else was around. This is the cycle of bondage and this is exactly where Satan wants you. He wants you to think that everyone will judge you and that you're the only one who is struggling. He wants you to believe that it should be kept secret and that sexual sin isn't something that you can talk about with other believers.

Think about how often we actually address this issue within our lives or talk to someone about it. It's easy to go to someone for prayer regarding direction, a job, or healing, but it's a little more difficult to admit you struggle with pornography. You find it awkward to ask someone to stand in agreement with you to be set free from masturbation. You can't fathom telling someone that you struggle with lesbianism while being active and involved in church. Oh, and you don't even want to have to think about admitting to someone that you're having sex with your little boo thang who you've posted pictures on Instagram with #CourtingGodsWay as the caption.

This is how it's so easy to remain in bondage to sexual sin. It's one of the biggest secret struggles that people have, and it's easy to hide. Since we don't talk about it, it just gets swept under the rug all while we struggle with deeply rooted bondage that goes unaddressed. We convince ourselves that simply because it shouldn't be an issue for us, it will eventually just go away.

It doesn't.

It remains within our hearts as we wrestle with living a life that is in constant conflict with what we portray to everyone else. We'll continue to hold on to this secret, not just because we don't want other people to know our business, but sometimes it's because we enjoy it. We don't want to share it and then have to deal with conviction. We enjoy the temporary pleasure we receive and to give it up is not always something that is easy, even when we know it goes against who we are aiming to be in God.

Just as with all the other topics we've discussed, you also have to identify your *why* when it comes to sexual sin. Why do you find yourself falling into the same trap time and time again? What is it that sex does for you? Is that what makes you feel loved? Does it fill a void within your life where you're longing for intimacy? Does it make you feel like you have some sense of control? What draws you to watch pornography? Do you really want to be delivered from it, or do you enjoy it? Only *you* can identify your *why*; if you can't face it when it's just you, this book, and God, you'll be less likely to face it with your brothers or sisters in Christ.

We have to confront this secret within our lives because Satan uses it daily to detour us from our God-given purpose. He knows that no other sin impacts the body like sexual sin (1 Corinthians 6:18). That is why we're told to "run from sexual sin," but often we find ourselves slowly turning towards it as we invite lust into the depths of our heart (1 Corinthians 6:18). We'll ignore it though, because it's just little stuff here and there.

It's always *little stuff.*

It always starts off small.

A little thought here. A little flirting there. A little touching here. Then before you know it you done went half on a baby and you're like wait, how did this happen?!

We're always surprised when consequences present themselves, but we will constantly ignore every single warning that came before then. The reality is, you don't fall into temptation overnight. It's a process of seeds being planted that are never uprooted. We fail to see that temptation is always present and we have to be alert and aware of this. This is so important because temptation in itself is not sin; it's when you give in to temptation that it becomes a sin. If you can learn how to guard your mind and heart from temptation when it presents itself, you will be able to fight against the tactics of the enemy when he tries to plant the seed.

First Corinthians 10:13 reminds you that when you face temptation "God is faithful. He will not allow the temptation to be more than you can stand. When you are tempted, he will show you a way out so that you can endure." He will always provide a way out, but you have to take that way out! That doesn't mean you wait until you are butt naked in the bed to say "Jesus, if I'm not supposed to have sex with this person, I need You to put my clothes back on supernaturally!" Honey child, I promise you the way out was provided before you made it through the door.

Too often, we ignore all the opportunities He provides as the way out as we push the boundaries a little further time and time again. We'll rely on will power to be our means to remain pure, only to find ourselves falling into the same traps. We may feel as though we can handle certain things, but we don't realize how it opens the door for temptation to walk right in.

We can even make the mistake of believing that simply because we're a believer, there's no way that we could ever end up entangled in sexual sin. Can we be completely candid for a moment? Of course, we can! Just because you love Jesus and stay in your Word, that does not eliminate natural urges, feelings, or desires. They will be present because the desire to have sex is completely a natural one. Sex itself is a natural act that God created. It was never designed to be evil, but it was created to be between a husband and wife within marriage (1 Corinthians 7:1-6).

Even as cute, saved, blessed, and highly favored as you are, you too can fall into the trap of sexual sin. Sometimes we can think we are more delivered from things than we really are, and we'll end up testing the limits as we convince ourselves that we can handle it. We assume we've been completely delivered because the signs aren't present anymore. This ends up being problematic because we make the mistake of confusing dormancy with deliverance. The thing about dormancy is that at some point, the issue will return. You may think you have been delivered when in reality, an opportunity just hasn't presented itself to reawaken what has been dormant. It's easier, not necessarily easy, to remain abstinent when you're single as a Pringle with no prospects in sight. What happens when that fine Christian man you prayed for is actually fine and now tangible?

We don't always think about these things. We believe that we love Jesus enough to help us to remain pure. It will definitely influence our decision to commit to purity, but we don't want to be naïve and believe the lie that being a follower of Christ will exempt us from sexual temptation and sin. If you don't deal with it and allow God to fully deliver you, it will become very present in your life.

Now you might be thinking, "Okay that's cute, but how do I tame this thing on the inside of me if I really want to honor God in this area?" Listen, I'm not even going to front and act as though it's easy. It can be challenging sometimes. As someone who has been abstinent for nine years, I've learned that purity is a daily choice. Making that choice is not necessarily the hard part; maintaining it is where the struggle comes in. It's easy to be pure initially. It's easy to be excited about your new purity journey when it's fresh and you're committed. But what happens when the feeling you had when you made the commitment is long gone? Are you able to maintain it? Are you able to still choose purity when everyone else around you is not? Are you able to stick to the commitment you made when temptation arises? These are things to think about.

Many times, we make decisions from an emotional place. We get caught up in a moment, we make emotional confessions at the altar, but when we leave, we leave our deliverance and healing there, too. After a few weeks, we find ourselves right back in the same traps that we've always run into and we wonder how we got there.

In some cases, we find ourselves committing to things simply because we jumped on a bandwagon of what seemed to be the "thing" to do. I loved that actress Meagan Good and her husband, Devon Franklin, were able to use their platforms to promote abstaining from sex before marriage. I truly think that was awesome, but it almost minimized the significance of purity. It was made into a trend because celebrities were doing it and it was misconstrued to be something that you do to get a spouse. Hear me clearly, I'm not blaming or shading them for that; they got a great message out to the public. The reason I bring it up is because when you do something simply because it's popular or with wrong motives, you're less likely to stick to it once the hype dies down.

Are you still going to be committed to purity six years later when you're still extremely single? Are you going to jump ship when your favorite Christian turns up pregnant out of wedlock? I'm not condemning that person, but too often we make the mistake of choosing to do, or not do, something based off a person and we fail to see that our commitment is rooted in everything but God. You see, one of the key components in maintaining purity is having the right foundation to your commitment to be pure.

So, what is your foundation? What is your reason for choosing purity? Now isn't the time to give your best politically Christian answer. It's okay to be honest about this. Is it because your parents pressed the issue and you don't want to disappoint them? Is it because you think it will quicken the process of getting a man? Is it because you truly want to honor God in all areas and live a life that is pleasing to Him? What is your why? If your why isn't rooted in God, it'll be so easy for it to be uprooted. You'll be swayed by what everyone else is doing or you'll give up when it doesn't appear to be benefiting you.

I remember when I was new in Christ and there were so many things that I was still on the fence about. I was fine with obeying God in certain areas, but I felt like others were old school and didn't apply to my generation. One of those areas was the topic of sex. I figured as long as I was in a committed relationship, or at least so I thought, then it wasn't a big deal if me and my boyfriend were having sex. I was serving in church, singing on the praise and worship team, saying hallelujah and amen, and having sex. I saw nothing wrong with it. I even invited the guy to church with me sometimes.

I would sit in church and listen to messages being preached about fornication and it went in one ear and out the other. I wasn't convicted because I didn't want to be. Truth be told, I enjoyed my lifestyle. I enjoyed having sex. It wasn't something that I felt I had to give up in order to serve God. It wasn't until I hit rock bottom in a relationship that I realized how tired I was of trying to do things my way. I didn't want to continue this pattern of failed relationships, only to end up at the same dead end—brokenness. It was after that relationship that I truly surrendered to the Lord and invited Him into my heart. The Holy Spirit began to show me that there's no such thing as riding the fence. I was either going to be on one side of it or the other. I was either for God or against Him. It was just that simple. There was no in between or grey area as I was trying to make it out to be.

It was at this time that I realized I wanted to honor God in this area, and not just because my bishop preached against fornication. It wasn't because I wanted to add it to the list of things that would make me feel super holy. A part of it was that I didn't want to be a hypocrite anymore. The bigger part was that I wanted to honor God in every aspect of my life. I no longer wanted to read His Word to pick and choose what I thought was acceptable based on whether or not I was willing to give it up.

I wanted Him to be my standard.

I needed Him to be my standard.

I *needed* the Word of God to be my standard.

In order to walk in purity, we have to be honest with ourselves about what the Bible says in regard to sexual temptation and sin. Notice I didn't say what we *think* it should say or what we *want* it to say. We have to take the Word for what it says without twisting it to fit into the box that makes us feel comfortable with what goes against what God said.

When we look at 1 Corinthians 6:9, Apostle Paul is talking to the church of Corinth and he tells them:

Don't you realize that those who do wrong will not inherit the Kingdom of God? Don't fool yourselves. Those who indulge in sexual sin, or who worship idols, or commit adultery, or are male prostitutes, or practice homosexuality, or are thieves, or greedy people, or drunkards, or are abusive, or cheat people—none of these will inherit the Kingdom of God.

I love when Paul gets a little sassy with the church! He pretty much tells them, *don't get it twisted.* You can choose to pick what parts of the Bible you like based off whether it convicts you or not if you want to, but it doesn't change what His Word says. You can't inherit the Kingdom of God if you have this sin in your life. You can't call yourself a follower of Christ but continue to willfully follow after and indulge in sin.

We have to be real about that.

Just as Paul said, "don't fool yourselves," you have to be honest in answering the question, are you fooling yourself? Are you convincing yourself that you can do whatever you want to as long as you go to church or open your Bible during the week? People will try to convince themselves that God will accept any and everything because He's a merciful and gracious God. He graces us not so that we can continue in sin, but to give us the opportunity to turn away from it so that we don't have to experience His wrath.

We often overlook sin that is considered acceptable or that has been normalized by the standards of this world. Since it's accepted by society, we become desensitized to it and we no longer view it to be an issue within our heart.

Romans 12:2 tells us,

> *Don't copy the behavior and customs of this world, but let God transform you into a new person by changing the way you think. Then you will learn to know God's will for you, which is good and pleasing and perfect.*

When we look at different aspects of the world, we can see that almost everything is overly sexualized. It is not uncommon to turn on basic cable and see a sex scene. Don't even get me started on music! I remember listening to songs back in the 90s and there were definitely a lot of sexual innuendos in songs, but it wasn't blatantly obvious. Nowadays, nothing is left to the imagination.

You can turn on the radio and hear play-by-play what a person is going to do, how they're going to do it, and how they're going to smack it, lick it, and drop it. It's always in your face whether you're looking for it or not.

This is why it is so important to allow the Lord to transform you from the inside out. It's necessary to allow Him to renew your mind daily because temptation is present daily. You can be sitting around minding your business, and out of nowhere, all kind of crazy thoughts will pop into your mind. You'll start thinking about no good Nathan and how although he was Satan's baby cousin in the flesh, he sure was fine though. Then you start listening to that song that always makes you think of him and reminds you of your pre-Jesus days, and now you're entertaining thoughts that you know you don't have any business thinking about.

I personally had to cut out a lot of TV shows, movies, and secular music because of how explicit they've become. There are certain things I cannot entertain, no matter how great others might think it to be, because I want to protect my purity. Since I am not a virgin, there are certain things that can trigger thoughts for me that can take my mind off all things Jesus quick and in a hurry. I have to be honest about that for myself because what is a conviction for me may not be for someone else. Some people can listen and watch certain things and it not impact them, but as for me and my eyes and ears, I have to be intentional about guarding them.

I've learned that an idle mind can be very dangerous. It allows thoughts to be planted that can easily go unchecked. What started off as something completely innocent can turn completely vivid in no time. That's what Satan is hoping will happen. He's hoping you won't think anything of the seeds that he attempts to plant, so that they can take root as they go unaddressed. You have the ability to fight against that! He may plant the seed, but you are the one who determines whether or not it gets watered. You are the one who has the ability to entertain it and allow different scenarios to play out in your mind. It's important to learn how to shut those thoughts down before they take root; otherwise, they just lay the groundwork for lust to seep in.

Once lust presents itself, temptation is always very close behind. It's lurking around waiting for any opportunity to grab a hold to you. When it does, it will convince you that nothing is wrong and no one will ever find out. As it takes root, it will lead you to believe that you should be able to do whatever you want to do. It's your body after all, so why shouldn't you do what you want? As you become more entangled in temptation, it'll be harder to recognize how you've become bound to your own desires. You won't even be able to see that you've become enslaved to your own flesh. Every time you get those *feelings* or get lonely, you give in to appease your flesh temporarily...one more time. You can't even see that you lack self-control and discipline because you're in bondage to yourself.

The reason I share that is because I've been there. I've been in that place where I was voluntarily remaining in bondage, but I couldn't see it. It wasn't until I realized that there were still areas that I had not completely surrendered to Christ, that the scales were removed from my eyes.

I have to ask you, have you really surrendered every area in your life to Him or have you silenced those that you don't want to think about? Are you truly surrendered, or are you trying to figure out how far you can push the boundaries without having sex, while still claiming to be a Christian? Are you willing to trust Him with your purity, or do you still feel like this is your body, this is your life, and you can do with it as you please? Your life is not your own. When Jesus died on Calvary, His blood paid the price for your life (1 Corinthians 6:19-20). Our bodies are a temple of the Holy Spirit as a result of this (1 Corinthians 6:19).

I want you to know that if you desire to be free, you can be. Just because you were, or still may be, entangled in sexual sin, it doesn't mean that you can't be redeemed.

It doesn't mean that you can't be holy and live a lifestyle that is pleasing to God. Too often we stay stuck in these cycles that we feel like we can't break free from. Who told you that you were stuck? Who told you that you couldn't stay out of the bed? Who told you that you have to remain in bondage because this is how it has been, so you can't break free from it?

God's grace and mercy says otherwise.

The blood of Jesus says otherwise.

No matter how deep or how long you've been in it, God can truly come in and deliver you from any bondage. The question is, do you *want* to be delivered? It's hard to allow God to deliver you from what you consider to be a secret struggle when the real secret is that you enjoy doing it. He will meet you where you want to be met, but it's up to *you* to be honest about that meeting place. He's inviting you to meet with Him in an honest place. He desires to heal and free you from the weight of sexual sin. Will you allow Him to take the reins? Will you trust Him with your purity and surrender your desires and wants to His will? He's calling you to a place of freedom and I pray that you will meet Him there.

Chapter 9
Rejection
What Do You Mean "No?"

→»)»»)————————————(((((((←

A few years ago, there was a guy who I really liked. After a couple of months of getting to know one another, we had the "Where is this going?" conversation. It was a pretty short talk.

He told me that he didn't want to be in a relationship.

Now, I played it cool on the phone, but in my head, I thought, "Wait, what just happened? He has me all the way messed up!" I'm relatively funny, depending on who you ask, I love Jesus and I feel like I look decent when my twist out is popping. Like how could he *not* want to be in a relationship with me? Regardless of what his reasoning was, I was rejected. It wasn't the first time and likely will not be the last.

Later that night, I sat before the Lord and told Him how frustrated I was. It wasn't just about the guy, but it was also about my pattern with men in general. Every relationship or situationship I've been in has always ended the same. They always start out with the guy showing lots of interest in me and putting forth effort. But they always ended with him not being ready, not wanting a relationship, or some other reason. I can't tell you how many times I've heard:

I like you, but...

You're amazing, but...

I think you're great, but...

There has always been a *but.* Quite frankly, my butt was over it. As I sat on the floor I told God, "I don't understand why they always change their mind about me." I felt like if I was kind enough, pretty enough, or funny enough, then that would *be* enough. But it never was. While I poured out my frustrations to God, He began to show me that I had allowed rejection to take root in my life and I needed to be freed from it.

Whenever you think of the word *rejection,* there's usually a specific incident that comes to mind. I'm sure you can think of a time when you felt like you weren't accepted, someone didn't approve of you, or didn't choose you. Maybe you experienced rejection from a man or the cool kids in school. Perhaps it was the dream job you got your hopes up for but didn't end up getting. Maybe it was the school you always wanted to go to that sent you a rejection letter. Or maybe it was the loan for the house, car, or business that you wanted, and even needed, that you were denied for.

Everyone experiences rejection in some form; it's inevitable. But rejection in itself is not the issue. It's the effects of rejection that go unaddressed that become problematic in our lives. It leaves us feeling insecure, questioning why we weren't good enough, and thinking that something is wrong with us. Nobody wants to be rejected, but it happens. When rejection goes unaddressed we can end up in bondage to it as we build up defense mechanisms to protect ourselves.

When you don't face the rejection that you've experienced, it starts to reveal itself in your relationships with others. You'll end up distancing yourself from people with the mindset of, let me reject you before you reject me. Instead of allowing people to get close to you, you build up a wall to keep everyone at an arms distance. When rejection has taken root, you don't even recognize that it's not healthy to constantly burn bridges because you view it as a means of protection.

Rejection doesn't just impact your relationship with people, but it also effects your relationship with God. You can end up pulling away from Him as you beat yourself up with condemnation. Part of this is because you become convinced that you can never be good enough or perfect enough for God. For some people, this is a result of being rejected by people in church as they were told what they couldn't do or be from people with a legalistic or traditional mindset. They then end up equating that to how God views them as well, even though that's not always the case.

Before you can overcome the effects of rejection, you must first identify that it's something you need to be freed from. It's easy to overlook the signs that the root of your behavior is from rejection when you don't view your actions to be problematic. It's important, however, to identify what kind of fruit is being produced in your life, because that reflects who the sender is. The Holy Spirit will produce fruit in our lives that reflects, "love, joy, peace, patience, kindness, goodness, faithfulness, gentleness, and self-control" (Galatians 5:22-23). Whereas, our sinful nature produces, "sexual immorality, impurity, lustful pleasures, idolatry, sorcery, hostility, quarreling, jealousy, outburst of anger, selfish ambition, dissension, division, envy, drunkenness, wild parties, and other sins like these" (Galatians 5:19-21).

I came across an article online from Above and Beyond Christian Counseling that identified the following as indicators that a person is struggling with rejection:[1]

- You find yourself comparing your circumstances or situations with others, and you never seem to measure up.

- You feel like you missed out on life's opportunities and now it's too late.

- No amount of encouragement is enough to convince you of your worth.

- You feel rejected if you are not greeted or acknowledged by leadership.

- You constantly seek the approval of others and suffer from people pleasing.

- You are easily offended or embarrassed from discipline or correction.

- You are always trying to prove yourself in public.

- You feel like you are on the outside looking in during interactions with people.

- You think you could do a better job than the current leader or teacher if you are given the opportunity.

- You believe no one understands you or what you are going through.

This list is not all-inclusive, but it gives you a starting point for further self-examination. As you discover the indicators of rejection, understand that they are merely a reflection of what has taken root. Don't simply focus on the fruit that was produced from rejection, but also identify the seed that took root and what allowed it to grow. There's always a root attached to rejection and tackling the behavior without addressing the root barely allows you to scratch the surface of the issue.

The Lord had to show me that the root of my rejection stemmed from my father. I remember watching the show *One on One* when I was younger, and wishing I had a relationship with my dad like Flex and Breanna had. Although my parents were married for multiple years, I was never a daddy's girl. After they divorced, our relationship became even more distant as I rarely saw or spoke to him. Even though I had forgiven my father and moved forward, I never really dealt with everything that I felt regarding our situation. God had to remind me that the first man who I felt changed their mind or who was unsure about me was my father.

I knew this, but I didn't want to admit it because I didn't want to be the girl with daddy issues. I didn't want to acknowledge that the thought crossed my mind on multiple occasions of not just why he wasn't more present, but why he didn't choose to be. It was hard for me to admit that as a child, I wondered, "Was it something about me that he didn't want?" Although he has made amends and I don't hold it against him, there were still a lot of emotions attached to this part of my life that I had allowed to go unaddressed.

Identifying the root of your rejection is what opens the door for healing to begin to take place. Initially, you might want to avoid doing so because it may require you to revisit some painful memories. Trust that God will walk you through it and know that His purpose in doing so is not to hurt you but to free you; to free you of disappointment, anger, resentment, frustration, and rejection. It's a necessary step to move forward, because otherwise you'll get stuck in a cycle that keeps pointing back to yourself.

As we discussed in chapter three, it can be difficult to fully walk in freedom in Christ when you have a mistaken identity. To overcome rejection, you must correct that mistaken identity. Where rejection tells you that you aren't good enough, you're inadequate, or you're overlooked, you have to correct that mindset with what God says about you. It's difficult to cast down thoughts that don't line up with the Word of God when you don't know the Word for yourself. Take the time to look at scriptures that tell you who you are to, and in, God. This is important because when you know who you are in Him, it also helps you to recognize who and what you are *not*.

When you feel like you've been discarded, rendered as useless, or cast out, rest in the same truth that God spoke over Jeremiah: "I knew you before I formed you in your mother's womb. Before you were born I set you apart" (Jeremiah 1:5). Before you were ever rejected, you were chosen. You were thought of and called by God before you were ever an afterthought to anyone else. Even if your parents didn't want you, God adopted you into His family (Ephesians 1:5). This verse even tells us that "this is what he *wanted* to do, and it gave him great pleasure." People may have rejected you, but God always wanted you. It gave Him great pleasure to have you as one of His daughters. First Peter 2:9 tells you that, "you are a chosen people. You are royal priests, a holy nation, God's very own possession." I love the reminder that He chose us. We have not always chosen Him, but He has always chosen us.

When I was ready to deal with my rejection, I sat on the floor and cried out to God. He began to remind me of Steffany Gretzinger's song *No Longer a Slave*. I had watched a video on YouTube of her singing this song and there's a part where she says, "We can be confident because He's sure about us. He's confident in His choice." That particular part was what replayed in my mind. The Lord began to show me that although, men and other people had changed their mind about me, He had not. Not only had He not changed His mind but He was confident in His choice in me from day one. He still chooses me today.

Regardless of the rejection you have encountered, God still chooses you. Not only has He chosen you, but He'll also free you from rejection and still use it to work out to your benefit. A lot of times when we're faced with rejection, we only focus on the negative aspects of it, but we fail to see how it can position us for something greater.

Take Rahab for instance; when we meet her in Joshua 2, she is labeled as the harlot who two spies encounter as they're scoping out the land of Jericho that the Israelites are getting ready to invade. Since she was a known prostitute, it's safe to assume that she had a reputation throughout the town. Prostitutes were considered to be unclean and the consequence of most sexual impurity required a person to be stoned (Leviticus 19:29; Deuteronomy 22:13-30). I could imagine that Rahab was looked down upon, treated like a misfit, and likely rejected. The women in the town probably referred to her as one of them "fast tail" girls. She probably wasn't invited to mid-day tea or for a Netflix and pajamas sleepover.

When we continue to read about her, we learn that her house was positioned on the town wall which made it an ideal location for the two spies to get into Jericho without being noticed (Joshua 2:15). Because of her being located there, her and her family were spared when the Israelites conquered the land. Understand that you can be rejected by people, but God can position you in the place that you need to be to spare your life. Despite rejection, He can still position you in places that no one else thought you deserved.

You see, Rahab's story doesn't just end in the book of Joshua. If we go over to Hebrews 11, we see Rahab's name mentioned again. Just to give you a little background on Hebrews 11, it's the chapter on faith. You could even consider it the faith hall of fame because the people who are mentioned were known for their great faith. As we read through this list, we see Abraham, Jacob, Moses, and others, but we also see our girl Rahab amongst the honorable mentions. It tells us that, "It was by faith that Rahab the prostitute was not destroyed with the people in her city who refused to obey God" (Hebrews 11:31).

I love that she's still labeled as a prostitute. Just hear me out! I love it because although she is labeled as a prostitute, her identity was now in being a woman of faith. What once was her identity, had been re-established in who she was in God, not what people rejected her for. We often get frustrated when we're dealing with rejection, but we don't realize that the people who rejected us aren't doing anything more than positioning us for where God is taking us. We keep getting mad at how people treat us when they reject us, but Psalm 110:1 tells us that the Lord will make our enemies our footstool. Don't allow the impact of rejection to hinder you from seeing that those who rejected you are really aiding in elevating and positioning you for greater.

It's easy to get distracted by the effects of rejection to the extent that we don't recognize how rejection has the potential to birth some amazing things. Let's go back to Rahab for a moment. I discovered something about little miss Rahab that completely caught me by surprise. I learned that she eventually had a son. I figured this out when I saw that her story didn't just end in Joshua or Hebrews, but that she's also mentioned in Matthew 1:5.

Now this caught me by surprise before I even flipped to the verse, because I knew that chapter was a genealogy of Jesus' ancestors. But when I read and saw, "Salmon was the father of Boaz (whose mother was Rahab)" I almost threw the whole Bible! Can we talk about how rejection can birth some amazing things?!

Just in case you're not familiar with Boaz, his story is found in the book of Ruth. He is the man who all us single women are told to wait for. He's pretty much the prototype of a *good* man. He was successful and a man of wealth and prestige. He took the widow Ruth as his wife and took care of her mother-in-law. There's no description of his physical characteristics, but I'm just going to add the icing to the cake and say that he was fine, too. This was a great man, and his mother was a former prostitute. I love it!

It gets better. Ruth and Boaz have a son who they name Obed and he is the father of David (Ruth 4:21-22). Yes, that would be King David, the one who defeated Goliath (1 Samuel 17). Who would've thought that Rahab, the misfit, the prostitute, the fast girl, would be an ancestor of both King David and Jesus Christ?

God always has a way of taking those people rejected and using them so that He can get the glory. Sometimes you miss this though, when you don't see what is on the other side of rejection. You don't see what is on the other side of the people who walked out of your life, but God has a way of sprinkling a whole lot of Romans 8:28 over your situation. I'm talking about in a way that He even allows rejection to work out for your good.

And we know that all things work together for good to them that love God, to them who are the called to his purpose (Romans 8:28, KJV).

For some people ministries will be birthed from the rejection they've experienced. Businesses will be birthed from the doors that were closed and all the no's that were given. Generations of Bible believing, prayer warrior, not today Satan, and try me not children will be birthed from rejection. But the enemy has a way of convincing you that rejection will leave you broken, empty, and frustrated. You must recognize that rejection is not a dead end. Instead, it protects you and positions you for impact and purpose.

When we look back at Rahab, we see that she asked the spies to spare her and her family's lives when the Israelites conquer the land because she had hidden them when the King of Jericho sent his men looking for them (Joshua 2:2-7). The two spies told Rahab that her house would be spared as long as she had a scarlet thread hanging outside her window (Joshua 2:17-18). It was the scarlet thread that would seal the agreement, so when the Israelites invaded Canaan, they knew not to kill Rahab and her family—even though she technically was deserving of death like the rest of the Canaanites.

The thing about scarlet is that it is a red color. When I see it, I can't help but to think about the blood of Jesus. It's the blood of Jesus that God sees when Satan comes to tell Him about everything we've done wrong and how we're deserving of death because of the sin in our lives. It's the blood of Jesus that God sees that spares our lives.

Christ became rejection for you and me so that we didn't have to be rejected by God. He was rejected by His own people, the Jews, and rejection was what positioned Him for the cross. The cross positioned Him for His blood to be shed. I'm referring to the blood that cleanses us from all unrighteousness. The blood that washes away our sins. The blood that gives us strength. I'm talking about the blood that still works.

The blood positioned Christ for His death, and His death positioned God to raise Him from the grave three days later. Jesus' rejection was used to restore us back to God and don't you think for one second that He won't use the rejection you've encountered and work it out in your favor. I know closed doors are never easy and sometimes it can be difficult to understand why you didn't get the job, why people left you, why you were denied for the loan, and just *why* in general. But know that God will use rejection to set you up for your rightful position in due season.

Chapter 10
Becoming
Who I Am vs. Who I Want to Be
→))))))))⟶⟵(((((((((⟵

Throughout my walk with Christ, I've found myself wrestling with the dichotomy of not being where I used to be, but also not being where I want to be. God has done such a great work within me and I could never even attempt to take credit for it, but I'm often reminded of how there's still so much work to be done. I'm always trying to get to that place where I feel like I have some type of hold on my life. I want to be able to know what's going on, make all of the right decisions, and have everything figured out!

A girl can hope, right?

I'm constantly trying to make sense of what God is doing in my life and every time it seems like I might have life figured out, God's like, "let me hit her with that new-new right quick and switch things up!" Oh, and don't even get me started on when you get to a place where you start to feel even a little bit comfortable with who you've become. Nah. Just because you're comfortable it doesn't mean that God has finished His work in you. There's more, don't you worry!

I could go on and on about the different components of the struggle to becoming the person God created you to be, but one of the biggest struggles is being right in the middle of that process. You aren't who you used to be but you also haven't made it to the place that God is leading you. The reason this becomes a struggle is because it's easy to become fixated on three aspects to the process of becoming:

1. Who you currently are
2. Who you want to be
3. Who you portray yourself to be

This can be a daily struggle for many because they look at where they are in relation to where they want to be, and they know there's so much for them to pursue than what's before them. Maybe that sounds familiar as you find yourself at a job that you're completely miserable and unfulfilled at. Or you're sitting in class, or studying to get into school, all while wondering, "Is it *really* important for me to get this degree?" Better yet, you started the business, blog, ministry, or whatever else by faith and it didn't take off how you thought it would at all. You believe everything that has been spoken over you, but in comparison to what you currently see and experience, it's just not adding up. You look at your life and whether you say it out loud or not, there's a part of you that thinks, "God, this can't be it! It just can't be."

Something equally challenging is when God has shown you how He's going to use you in all these amazing ways and He's given you vision for days, but there's no fruit of it yet. Maybe He's shown you the name of the ministry you will have, the job you're going to get, or the family member who will give their life to Christ. All these things have been spoken over you, for years even, but you're not in the place to see it come to fruition yet. I understand the frustration that comes with this, because you desire to get to that place and be who you're striving to be, but you aren't there yet.

A lot of times in our walk with Christ, the part of our journey that we get stuck in is the middle. It's the part of the transition where we're faced with the reality of who we are in comparison to who we want to be. In the midst of this, there's the dilemma of how we choose to portray ourselves as we're going through that transition. You might think that who you are would line up with who you portray yourself to be, but that often isn't the case.

We've become a people who have done a great job of portraying ourselves to be someone we are not. You have people who will buy expensive cars and clothes, take extravagant trips, and eat at the fanciest of restaurants just for others to see. Listen, I can appreciate a good "treat yourself" moment, but the problem lies in doing all of this just for the sake of show. What good is it to portray that you're *keeping up with the Joneses* when in reality you're living on a *Good Times* budget? There are tons of people living in significant debt as they try to portray an image of something they are currently not.

It's no different in church, either. We will praise and worship with the best of them, then go home and struggle with addictions, depression, pornography, and other issues that we keep hidden beneath the façade that appears during church attendance. Now, I'm not condemning the person who comes to church and struggles with real issues. We all have mess in our closets and some of our mess makes it to our front door. The issue with it is that it's difficult to be delivered from what you pretend doesn't exist.

The issue with pretending is that it's not necessarily the person's lifestyle or the issue that keeps them in bondage. It's their need to cover their truth with what they pretend to be. This is an area that the Holy Spirit has had to deal with me on, on a number of occasions. As a woman who likes to look a certain way, God has shown me that sometimes as women we can feel as if we look put together on the outside, then it will distract people from realizing how messed up we are on the inside. If we can portray a presentable image for people to see, it won't cross their mind that we could possibly be broken, struggling, hurting, and confused beneath the layers that they can see.

That's exactly what is happening with people in the body of Christ today. They have the desire to grow in their walk, but they aren't yet where they want to be in their relationship with Christ. So, they just pretend to have it together.

They pretend to know the Word of God.

They pretend to live holy.

They do all of this pretending that they become so entangled in presenting this image of living for Christ that they fail to see that they never truly developed a relationship with Him. Instead they remain stuck and bound. They never deal with the very thing that is hindering them from growing as they pretend that it doesn't exist. It saddens me to think about how many people identify themselves as believers but will end up missing heaven because they spent more time pretending to be a follower of Christ than truly cultivating a relationship with Him. We have to move past this because we will never get to where we want to be or even where

God wants us to be by portraying ourselves to be something we are not.

I love Philippians chapter three, because Apostle Paul gives us a new perspective on the way that we think about the process of becoming all that we are to be. Oftentimes, you'll hear people quote the infamous verse from this chapter, "I press toward the mark for the prize of the high calling of God in Christ Jesus," but we miss that Apostle Paul drops some serious knowledge prior to this verse (Philippians 3:14, KJV). He talked about some desires that he had, but in order for us to understand his desires, we must understand Paul's history, which he outlines first.

He starts off the chapter stressing the importance of understanding that neither circumcision nor anything else a person can do can save them; salvation is found solely in accepting Jesus Christ as Savior (Philippians 3:2-3). This is important to note because in the Old Testament, circumcision was the sign that a person was a part of God's covenant (Genesis 17:9-14). The problem with this was that circumcision was to be a reflection of keeping the Lord's commands, but instead, Israel was extremely disobedient. They were circumcised in the flesh, but their heart revealed that they didn't truly have a relationship with God.

Right after Paul talks about how there is nothing that makes us deserving of salvation, he pretty much drops his resume explaining how if anyone had the credentials to save themselves, he would be the person (Philippians 3:4). Now if you read that verse alone, you might think that Paul is being mad cocky but there is a significant purpose in him sharing this.

Let's break this down right quick!

First, Paul hits us with how he was circumcised when he was fresh out of the womb at eight days old (Philippians 3:5). Then he says, "I am a pure-blooded citizen of Israel" (Philippians 3:5). In other words, his ancestry.com results came back and confirmed he was from the nation of Israel. He's legit! But wait, there's more! He says he was "a member of the tribe of Benjamin" (Philippians 3:5).

Pause.

This actually holds some weight. He's not just name dropping like, "I'm from the tribe of my momma and daddy." No one would care. But to say he was from the tribe of Benjamin was significant because Israel's first king, Saul, came from this tribe and their heritage was respected by the Jews (1 Samuel 10:20-21). He was also a Pharisee, and Pharisees were known for their devotion to the Jewish law (Philippians 3:5). To top it off, Paul persecuted Christians because he thought they were committing blasphemy by accepting Jesus as the Son of God, and he thought he was honoring God in doing so (Philippians 3:5). Last but certainly not least, he states how obedient he was to the law of God that he basically could've been considered blameless (Philippians 3:5).

After he drops all of his credentials, he then says:

I once thought these things were valuable, but now I consider them worthless because of what Christ has done. Yes, everything else is worthless when compared with the infinite value of knowing Christ Jesus my Lord (Philippians 3:7-8).

Did you catch the shift that just took place? Paul went from talking about what could justify him, to looking at Christ alone. The purpose of him sharing all of that about himself was not to brag by any means. It was to show that none of that mattered in comparison to knowing Jesus. In spite of how impressive his credentials were, it was nothing but the grace of God that saved him. Now that the focus has been taken off of him, we're able to look at the desires he had in a new light. As we continue to read, there are three desires that Paul speaks of:

1. That he may gain Christ (Philippians 3:8)
2. That he may become one with Christ (Philippians 3:9)
3. That he may know Christ (Philippians 3:10)

Right after he shares these desires, he acknowledges that he is not perfect. He has not yet gotten there, but he's striving to get there (Philippians 3:12).

Mind you, we started off talking about the three struggles of who we are, who we want to be, and who we portray ourselves to be. Could it be that these things become a struggle because our goals and desire for our life are out of order? Could it be that we have become so consumed about self that we've forgotten to ask the question, "How can I be more like Jesus?" Could it possibly be that the real areas to focus on aren't who we are, who we want to be, or who we portray ourselves to be but it's that we may win Christ, be found in Him, and know Him?

I love Apostle Paul's authenticity in this chapter because he acknowledges that even he had not obtained that place in his relationship with Christ, but he gives insight to what he does while he's pursuing his goal of getting there. He says, "but this one thing I do, forgetting those things which are behind, and reaching forth unto those things which are before, I press toward the mark for the prize of the high calling of God in Christ Jesus" (Philippians 3:13-14, KJV).

In order to press toward the mark, it requires us to endure on our way *to* the mark. Too often we have a tendency to give up or to get distracted in the middle.

Instead of continuing to go forward, we easily get discouraged at any sign of opposition that may get in the way. What we miss in this moment is that the opposition can be used to stretch us in order to help us finish the race.

I learned this lesson in 2015, when I signed up for a 5k with a few of my co-workers. I had done a few 5ks before, but this was the first time I signed up with the intention to actually run. Anyone who knows me well knows I'm sort of not about that exercise life, but I'm *definitely* not about the running life. I have an irrational, but very legit, fear of running on a treadmill, flying straight off into a wall, it being recorded and going viral on YouTube. Nonetheless, I was encouraged, or bamboozled, to run in this race.

The day of the 5k arrives and I go to the table to check in and get my number. The volunteer made a comment about how I looked like a runner. Of course I just smiled and said, "thank you." In my mind I'm thought, "HA! I'm about to run this steak and cheese in my mouth when this is over." I forgot to mention, there was a dinner that was promised after the race. I was all here for tearing up a steak and cheese on someone else's dollar.

The horn blows and we all take off running. As I start off, I have a good pace going. I feel like I've got it! I started to slow down about halfway through but then I realized there were people behind me so at least I wasn't in last place. I finally finish the first mile and I'm like, "oh snap, Jackie Joyner-Kersee, I'm coming for your title, girl!"

I wasn't.

Not even a little bit.

Apparently, I needed to be humbled, because a burning sensation started to grow in my chest and then my legs began to feel like they were at their end. On top of this, it started raining. My mind was convinced that I was Jackie's protégé in the making, but my body said, "so you thought." By the time I got to mile three, I had given up on my track star dreams. My run had diminished from a nice jog, to a brisk walk, to a limp, to me wondering if I could crawl to my car.

As I had maybe ten minutes left in the race, I looked up and I saw someone running in the opposite direction. I was confused but I just assumed that I was delusional at this point. Once the person got closer, I realized that it was one of my coworkers. She had already finished the race and she came back to help me finish mine. She ran with me from where I was all the way to the finish line, and the whole time she was cheering me on, reminding me that I could do it. I wanted to cry in that moment, but I didn't because #thuglife. But that meant more to me than she could've ever imagined; even more than the steak and cheese.

When I got back home that night, the Lord began to show me how the Holy Spirit is similarly coaching me through this race called life. As I'm pressing toward the finish line of eternity, He's there to encourage, challenge, and push me to finish the race. He's reminding me that I can do it if I just keep my eyes fixed on Jesus.

As I'm becoming all of who God created me to be, I may encounter some hills, storms, and I may even slow down at times. I may question the direction that I'm going, and I might even question if it is worth it. The thought might cross my mind that I may not make it and that I'm not cut out for it. I might even think about how who I am seems so far from who I want to be, that it appears to be unattainable. But when I shift my focus from it being about me, and I replace it with Christ, I'm then able to release the pressure in exchange for His presence. And in His presence, there is freedom (2 Corinthians 3:17); freedom from pretending, freedom from expectations, freedom from the weight of this world, and freedom to recognize that although I'm not where I want to be, with Christ, I will continue to strive to get there.

When we replace our focus from the struggle of who we are, who we want to be, and who we portray ourselves to be, with gaining Christ, being found in Him, and knowing Him, we're then able to adjust to what He is doing in us. As our focus shifts, we can take rest and find encouragement for this race in three ways:

1. The Father God
2. The Son Jesus
3. The Holy Spirit

No matter the wait, distance, or opposition of the transition, I want to encourage you to stay the course. Continue to press toward the mark knowing that God loves you and desired to have a relationship with you so much that He gave His only Son Jesus to die for you so that He could be close to you. Now you can run this race knowing that it is not in vain because Jesus' death and resurrection gives you the hope of eternity.

Allow the Holy Spirit that is within you to lead, guide, teach, comfort, and help you all the way to the day that Jesus returns for His church. Don't lose sight of the mark; it's worth pressing towards. It may not seem like it when you feel stuck in the middle for what seems like forever, but stay the course. Just because things aren't going as you planned, doesn't mean that they aren't going according to His plans. Keep pressing, keep striving, and keep becoming all that He created you to be.

Chapter 11
Elevation
It Sure is Lonely Up Here

E veryone wants to be elevated and grow deeper in the Lord, but oftentimes, they fail to take into consideration that it comes with a price. When you think about people who have an amazing anointing on their life, I can 100% guarantee you they have a testimony worth listening to. People are always amazed by the gifts, vision, and calling on someone's life, but most of the time, they have no idea what was and is required of that person to achieve their level of influence.

As you grow in your relationship with God, so much changes. You're stripped of so many things and you're placed in situations to develop different fruits of the spirit within you. You leave your comfort zone, and sometimes it can feel like you're in the middle of the ocean with no life jacket. You're excited as the Lord begins to reveal more to you through His Word, but you're trying to make sense of a lot of it at the same time.

You'll have some amazing moments when God gives you vision and you see His faithfulness working in your life. You'll be able to testify of Him being a provider, deliverer, healer, way-maker, and the one true living God. But there will also be times where you don't understand what is going on in your life. You'll question what you're doing wrong, if you misheard God, or if what was promised will really come to pass. Even as the Lord provides and shows you that He's with you, life has a way of trying to break your spirit to leave you in a place of discouragement and loneliness.

One of my favorite characters in the Bible who I believe could relate to this struggle was Elijah. He was such an amazing man of God. The way that God chose to use him still leaves me in awe every time I read about him. What I love most about Elijah is that although he had a number of amazing victories in God, we're able to see him have a very vulnerable moment in 1 Kings 19. At the beginning of the chapter, Elijah is on the run for his life and he's even reached a depressed stated. As he sits under a tree, he prays to the Lord that he might die as he cries out, "I have had enough! Lord, take my life" (1 Kings 19:4, CSB).

I have to give you the backstory in order for you to really understand the significance of this moment Elijah is having. Some pretty amazing things took place right before Elijah found himself in this place. For starters, when a drought took place in Israel, the Lord not only led Elijah to a brook with a steady source of water, but He also sent a raven to provide him with food (1 Kings 17:1-7). From there, the Lord led Elijah to Zarephath where he was able to see God provide for a woman who had run out of food due to their being no rain for the crops to grow (1 Kings 17:8-16). On top of that, the woman's son became ill and died, and the Lord heard Elijah's prayer and revived her son (1 Kings 17:17-24).

Don't get me wrong, all of that is beyond cool beans, but the main thing that Elijah is known for is the jaw-dropping, in your face, smack down of all times that he had on Mount Carmel. I'm talking about the moment where he stands as one man, completely solo-dolo, against the 450 prophets of Baal and the 400 prophets of Asherah, in a battle to see whose God was going to show up and show out (1 Kings 18:19-20). Now Baal and Asherah were false gods that the people had been worshipping under King Ahab and Queen Jezebel. So, Elijah tells the false prophets to gather wood together; they would call on their god, Baal, and Elijah would call on the Lord. Whichever god answered by fire would be known as the true God (1 Kings 18:22-24).

After the false prophets made a complete fool of themselves for hours by calling on Baal and getting no response, Elijah calls on the almighty God once. Immediately, the Lord sent fire down from heaven that consumed all of the wood, stones, dust, and water (1 Kings 18:36-38). After this, Elijah had all of the false prophets killed, then he prayed for rain, and the Lord strengthened him (1 Kings 18:40-46). Go on Elijah with your bad self!

But hold up, right after the very moment we read about Elijah being victorious in God, we get to chapter 19 and we find him fearful and depressed as he runs to Mount Sinai (1 Kings 19:3-4). Let me explain; since he killed all of Queen Jezebel's prophets, word on the street was that she wanted Elijah dead. So, he threw up the deuces and went in the complete opposite direction of her (1 Kings 19:1-3). Isn't it amazing how this man who had literally just called down fire from heaven so boldly in front of 850 false prophets, became fearful and ran because of one woman? Isn't it amazing how some of your weakest moments can come directly after your greatest victories in God?

Have you ever been in a place where you were on what felt like a spiritual high? You received a great Word or

God elevated you in your purpose. You went to a revival and got filled, healed, set free, and delivered. You cried out to the Lord, completely surrendered to Him, and He began using you for His glory.

But then life happened.

Reality set in after the spiritual high, and it's almost like you completely forgot what God *just* did.

That's where Elijah was. Just like him, there are moments where we'd rather run than face what is before us. No matter how anointed we are, how called we are, or how chosen we are, we experience that moment where it feels like *too much.* I can't speak for you, but I can say for myself that there have been a number of occasions where I haven't felt cut out for what is before me. There have been multiple times where I've considered giving up only to realize that I don't have anything to return back to. Each time, I've found myself pondering the same question that the Lord posed to Elijah: *What are you doing here?* (1 Kings 19:9).

You see, when Elijah fled from Jezreel to get away from Queen Jezebel, he didn't just go across the street. It took him forty days to get to Mount Sinai, which was over 200 miles away, and once he got there, he stayed in a cave (1 Kings 19:9). So, you can understand why God asked Elijah what he was doing there.

I want to pose the same question to you: what are you doing here?

When I say *here*, I'm referring to the place you are in life right now—whether it's at your job, school, mentally, spiritually, or whatever *here* might be for you. What are you doing here? Are you in the place that you're supposed to be in during this season, or are you running from your assignment? Are you running from the responsibility that God has given you because you've been faced with opposition? Are you running from committing to the call on your life simply because it comes with a price? What are you doing here?

It's important to ask yourself what you're doing in the place that you are in, because it will help you to identify what led you there. When we look at Elijah for example, we see that God led him to the brook during the drought, the widow's house in Zarephath, and to Mount Carmel. In every instance, we can see how the Lord provided for Elijah. But when Elijah got word that Queen Jezebel wanted to fight him on-site, fear is what led him to Mount Sinai, not God.

When our focus shifts away from God, we allow our emotions to dictate our direction instead of Him. For a lot of people, their emotions have put them in places that they aren't supposed to be in. They'll stay in places far too long simply because it's comfortable. They'll avoid going to places they need to because it's unfamiliar. They'll prolong accepting the calling on their life because it requires too much of them.

When you take your focus off of God, it's easy to get sidetracked by what you feel and don't feel like doing on any given day. Then, you'll find yourself in the same position as Elijah—feeling frustrated and alone because you were led by your emotions instead of the direction of the Lord.

When God asked Elijah why he ran to the cave, his response was,

> *I have been very zealous for the Lord God of Armies, but the Israelites have abandoned your covenant, torn down your altars, and killed your prophets with the sword. I alone am left, and they are looking for me to take my life* (1 Kings 19:10, CSB).

Now don't get me wrong, Elijah had a very valid argument, but he didn't answer the question. Even though he had a point, there was one part that was inaccurate. God tells Elijah that there was still a remnant of people, 7,000 to be exact, who were not worshiping Baal and who were willing to serve Him (1 Kings:19:18). He was letting Elijah know that he wasn't as by himself as he thought he was. God had to remind Elijah that there were still faithful people in Israel.

Sometimes the emotions that you experience can lead you to believe that you are completely alone. Especially as you mature in your walk with Christ and it seems like you're being stripped of people left and right. It seems impossible to find any godly friendships and you feel like you're left to figure everything out on your own. Then you get to a point where you're depressed, frustrated, and tired, so you withdraw to a place, whether physically or mentally, to abandon it all. As God asks, "What are you doing here?" it's easy to give the same response that Elijah did.

God, I've been trying to do everything right and it seems like everyone who is doing wrong is better off.

I'm living for You and it feels like everything is falling apart right now.

God, I obeyed You. I did what You said, but it feels like I'm being punished and I don't understand.

All the other Christians seem so happy but I'm over here struggling to not give up.

I followed Your instruction God, but I've lost everything. I look crazy out here!

As this mindset begins to take over, it's easy to unpack where we are and have a pity party for one. But just as God reminded Elijah that he wasn't alone, we need that same reminder at times too.

There's such a misconception that because you're serving God, growing in Him, walking in purpose, and pursuing the vision that He has for you, that life becomes easier. There's this idea that because you're trusting Him by faith, all doubt, fear, and concern regarding the journey ahead become eliminated. As you encounter opposition, it can be easy to feel confused as to why it appears that you're the only one who is struggling when everyone else seems to be living their best purposeful life ever. You feel alone and by yourself, even when you may be surrounded by people.

I can almost guarantee you that if you were to sit down and have a conversation with any believer who you think has a perfect Christian life, you would quickly learn that we all have different tests, trials, and hardships that we face. We may not always show it or talk about it openly with everyone, but you'd be surprised by how many people would say, "me too" if you just have the conversation.

I am beyond grateful for how the Lord has developed and matured me over the last couple of years. I'm truly thankful for the ministry that He has given me and the anointing that is on my life, but I would be lying if I said any of it has come easy. The thing about being rooted in Christ, along with having a ministry, is that people have a tendency to pull on you more. They'll look to you for advice, spiritual guidance, prayer, and so much more. You struggle with finding the balance with being available to people while not necessarily being accessible to everyone for your own sanity. You'll pour into people, serve in different capacities, and give your all. Sometimes the people who you do that for will never support you, or they'll be the first ones to turn their back on you.

The thing about growth and elevation is that people tend to have an extremely inaccurate view of it. There's a misconception that because you have a title, platform, you lead, pray, worship, fast, etc., that you don't go through anything. Or if you do face any tests or trials, you just breeze through it while quoting scripture and skipping through the daises of life. You constantly have people asking you for advice or prayer, yet you're rarely asked how you can be prayed for. You have to deal with your own problems, struggles, temptations, and sin, yes sin, and still pour into others when you barely feel capable of pouring into yourself.

You give your all to people who complain.

You give your all to people who don't show up.

You give your all to people who criticize.

You can pray for a person and see them healed or freed from an area that you're also believing God for in your own life that hasn't happened yet. You can prophesy over a person and see things come to pass for them while you're waiting on God for instruction and direction for what's next for yourself. There are moments where you're praying for someone, ministering, leading worship, etc. when you're dealing with grief, brokenness, depression, and life just happening in general. Sometimes it might be easy to press through it, but there also may be days where you just don't have it in you. But there's a weight attached to your gifts and anointing, and it's not placed there by God. It's placed by people's expectations, and even your own, that leads you to feel like you have to put a smile on to hide your tears because no one wants to hear about the broken version of you.

I want to be so very clear that I am not complaining, but I've had to learn to be honest with my struggle in this because for way too long, I have pretended. I have put on in church and around church people because it seemed like everyone else who was growing in God seemed to be going through life so smoothly. It appeared that no matter what came their way, they tackled it head-on and floated on the clouds of grace.

That wasn't my story.

I was tumbling and falling head-first, and it all felt like too much. Just like Elijah, I felt like I was by myself. I wanted to escape it all and just disappear. I didn't feel like I could handle everything that was attached to the depth of my relationship with God. The more I grow in

Him, the more I'm stretched. At times, that stretch hurts me to my core. It feels like it's going to end in a snap as I buckle under the weight of it all. But God has to remind me that my purpose was never created to be a burden or to break me. In contrast, it was given as a gift to unravel who I created myself to be, in order for me to become undone to reveal who I was always meant to be through Him.

Let's go back to Elijah for a moment. After he pours out his frustration to God, the Lord instructs him to leave the cave and stand before Him on the mountain (1 Kings 19:11). Before he comes out of the cave, a windstorm hit, then an earthquake, and then a fire (1 Kings 19:11-12). But the Lord was not found in any of it. Instead, He was found in a still, gentle voice as He asked him again, "What are you doing here, Elijah?" (1 Kings 19:12-13, CSB).

Sometimes as we're growing deeper in the Lord and we're trying to determine where we're supposed to be or what we're supposed to be doing, we miss it because we end up looking for a sign instead of listening for a word. God didn't use the strong winds, earthquake, or fire to communicate to Elijah. It's not that He couldn't, but He chose to speak to him in a still, gentle whisper. A lot of times, we're waiting on a spectacular sign from the Lord to get us to move or to get us where we need to be. We're waiting for Him to give us a miraculous sign for us to go where He's told us to or to believe that we're where we're supposed to be. We'll read our Bible and say, "God, if You really want me to do this, then give me a sign."

God's like, *I already did. I gave you My Word. Read it, hear it, and apply it to your life.*

I love that as we read 1 Kings 19:11-13, we see that the action that got a response from Elijah was the still voice, not all the other antics. He didn't come out of the cave when all of the natural events were happening, but it was when He heard the voice of the Lord speak to him. Catch this—in order for Elijah to hear the still voice, he had to be still himself and listen.

Too often we find ourselves saying we want to grow deeper in the Lord and that we want more of Him, and we look for a sign to guide us. If we could just learn how to operate in the spirit of hush sometimes, we would be able to discern that God is always speaking. We just need to listen.

Are you allowing yourself to hear what God is trying to say to you, or has His voice been drowned out by all the noise and excitement of this world? Has His voice become stifled by your doubts, worries, and frustrations as you try to make sense of everything that is going on around you? Or is it difficult to hear Him because you're running from what He's called you to?

Running from what God has placed inside of you and what He has assigned you to will never change the assignment. After Elijah responded with the same answer a second time, God instructed him to go back the way he came (1 Kings 19:15). After all those miles he had walked, Elijah now had to turn around and go back to the place he ran from because there was still work to be done there. The assignment still remained even as Elijah was trying to get as far away from it as he could.

Maybe you find yourself trying to run from what God is doing in your life at this very moment because it seems too hard and quite frankly, it's not what you signed up for. You didn't think it would be this difficult and you didn't realize what all was attached to you really living a life surrendered to God. I want to encourage you with one key reminder from Elijah's story. Although God never told him to run away, He allowed Elijah to have his moment. After he ran away, an angel came to him and told him to eat and drink and the Lord gave him strength to make it the forty-day journey to Mount Sinai (1 Kings 19:5-8). God didn't tell Elijah to run, but He realized his discouraged and depressed state. He recognized that Elijah needed to have a period of rest to strengthen and restore him. Once he had this time, the Lord sent him back out.

You're going to have some moments where you've obeyed God, you're doing your best, you're walking by faith, and you're growing in Him, but you also feel discouraged and weary. There will be times where you feel empty, weakened, and tired, as you wonder if you're doing the right things because it seems like every time you make strides forward, it feels like you get kicked backward at the same time. I want you to know that God sees that, too. He knows and He acknowledges when you need that moment to be strengthened and restored. He will allow you to have that rest, but know that there is still work to be done.

As you're going deeper in your relationship with the Lord, don't get discouraged in your well doing (Galatians 6:9). I know it can be difficult at times to continue to press toward the mark when it feels like you're constantly missing the mark but keep pressing. Growing in Him is hard, but it's also so rewarding when you just allow Him to do what only He can do. As you fully surrender and allow Him into your heart, He will seriously blow your mind in the ways that He uses you. It won't always be easy, but I can guarantee that it's so worth it to be where He has called you to be.

As you look at where you currently are today, ask yourself, "What am I doing here?" Are you where you're supposed to be in God? Are you allowing Him to fully use you for His glory or are you fighting the process? Are you remaining in a place that has already served its purpose or are you running from the assignment that God has given you? To get to the place where you can boldly call on the Lord and believe that He will answer as Elijah did on Mount Carmel comes with a price. It will cost you something, but I can also assure you that avoiding it will also cost you something.

You can't afford to miss what God desires to do with you in this season. This is not the season to be distracted. This is the time to rise up, pursue holiness, and trust God like never before. Are you ready to complete the work that God has assigned to you?

Chapter 12
Freedom
I'm Free at Last

*F*reedom by Eddie James is probably one of my all-time favorite songs. Not simply because that man has a war cry like nobody's business, but it's just one of those songs that fills my heart with joy. My favorite part is the vamp when he sings, "No more shackles. No more chains. No more bondage. I am free." Ah, I get so excited every time I sing it!

Just think about exclaiming boldly that there are no more holds on your life. There's no more bondage holding you back because the devil is defeated and you can say with confidence, "I am FREE!"

Do you believe that statement to be true? Do you truly believe that freedom is within your reach? Satan would like to convince you that it is not and that it's just a *cute* song, but not a reality of what your life could be.

Didn't I tell you that the devil is a liar and a snatcher of edges?

He loves to use manipulation and deception to lead you to believe that freedom is available to everyone but you. He wants to convince you that Jesus' blood somehow has the power to cover every sin and issue except for the ones that you are struggling with. He's more than happy to fuel the thoughts of condemnation that tell you that God is disappointed in you and that you can't return to Him when you mess up. Don't believe the lies!

The Bible tells us,

> *there is no condemnation for those who belong to Christ Jesus. And because you belong to Him, the power of the life-giving Spirit has freed you from the power of sin that leads to death* (Romans 8:1-2).

Can we just have a thank-God-for-Jesus moment? It's because of Jesus that we are free from the power of sin and that we receive power through the Holy Spirit to help us live a life that is pleasing to God.

This doesn't mean that we are going to be perfect by any means! As long as we are here on this earth, we are going to be prone to our sinful nature. This isn't an excuse to give into sin and be dominated by our flesh, though. Jesus surely did not die for us to indulge our flesh and to choose to remain in bondage to sin (Galatians 5:1; Galatians 5:13).

God knew that we would be tempted by our sinful nature, and even give into sin at times, therefore He provided us with the Holy Spirit to lead and guide us in holy living (Romans 8:5-14). In addition to this, God extends His grace to us when we turn from our sin (Romans 5:20-21). Instead of being condemned and receiving the punishment we deserve, we can go boldly before the throne of grace with confidence knowing that Jesus has already paid our debt. We can receive God's grace when we go before Him with a repentant heart and confess our sins to Him.

Satan, however, would rather convince you that God is too angry with you for you to return to Him. The enemy wants to plant the seed that God won't forgive you this time because you said that last time would be the last time. He wants you to think that God is upset with you, so it's better to avoid communicating with Him because you're going to be overwhelmed by guilt and shame. These are all tactics to keep you in bondage!

Satan knows that freedom is attached to your confession. He is well aware that when you repent, God will forgive you and cleanse you from all unrighteousness

(1 John 1:9). He knows that you will be met with healing, peace, love, grace, mercy, and freedom. He wants you to feel like you can't turn to God because he knows that the longer you wait to do so, the deeper entangled in bondage you'll become. It won't even feel like you're in bondage; it will start off with small distractions, a little temptation here and there, and you won't think twice about it. He'll convince you that you're fine because you're still doing all the Christian *stuff*. You're going to church, you're posting scriptures on social media, and you even lift your hands during worship.

Understand that one of the things that Satan loves more than you being in bondage, is you being bound yet pretending like you aren't. It's a cycle that only allows him to keep you there even longer. By refusing to acknowledge where your heart really is, you become self-destructive as you attempt to mask your issues with good deeds and church attendance. No matter how much you pretend for others, the ache for wholeness and freedom will still be present. Pretending will only rob you of the peace and fullness that comes from walking in freedom.

I've learned that it's hard to walk like a free person when I'm spending more time trying to perfect the façade of someone who should be free. For the longest time, I didn't even realize how pretending while secretly struggling with different areas was a form of bondage in itself. This doesn't just apply to pretending to be holy, but it also relates to not sharing all our heart with God. There may be times when it feels like we're experiencing hell on earth and we're trying so hard to ignore the fact that we're discontent with our portion. We'll smile and say we're doing fine when deep down, we're wondering why God has allowed certain things to happen.

He has to strip me of this mindset regularly. He reminds me that He can handle my heart, including the parts that may be frustrated with His direction or instruction. Even recently, He showed me that He wanted me to be honest about my feelings towards my current season. Not for Him, because He already knows, but for myself. He showed me that there was a need to break free from pretending like I understand or enjoy the seasons that I need to go through.

You see, I've been on a faith journey for a year now. In October 2016, the Lord led me to quit my full-time job to be unemployed. Throughout this year, God has been faithful and He has provided, but this has been one of the hardest seasons that I've had to endure in quite some time. It has been extremely lonely and there's still so much that I don't understand. The truth is I have tried very hard to make sense of the different things that I've felt led to do and others that I don't. I can't tell you how many times I have quoted Romans 8:28 and reminded myself that the Lord always has a plan and that His plans are good. Even in speaking and knowing this, I don't always *feel* this. I know His plans are good, but they don't always feel good when I'm on a rough path that is preparing the way for those plans.

One night, I sat on my floor as worship music played. Within seconds, I felt the warmth of tears roll down my cheek. I didn't have a *reason* to cry, yet I couldn't help but weep. I sat silently through four songs as tears streamed down my face and onto the floor. I felt this overwhelming presence letting me know that it was okay. Not that it would be okay, but that it *was* okay. I cried harder because at that moment I realized something that I had been holding in for a while. I had suppressed it so deeply that I didn't even realize it was how I felt.

The Holy Spirit was showing me that it was okay to speak my truth. As I thought about what was getting ready to come out of my mouth, I was reminded again, *it's okay.*

"God, I'm tired of this season. I don't want to do this anymore."

Immediately after, I said, "God, I'm so sorry." I felt guilty for being upset in this season, because I know that He has a purpose for it. He stopped me in my downward spiral of guilt and shame. He reminded me that He already knew; He just desired my honesty. When I was honest with Him, I could be free from the burden of trying to be okay with everything that I didn't understand. I could accept that I don't have to understand His plans in order for them to work.

There's so much freedom in being honest with the Lord. He can accept the parts of you that even the closest of people you know would reject. He can handle your truth. When you start to get real and honest with the Lord, you're drawn into an intimate place with Him. You'll see that you can be vulnerable with Him and He won't hold it against you. You'll see that even when it gets messy, He won't abandon you. You'll see that where the spirit of the Lord is, there truly is freedom (2 Corinthians 3:17).

This freedom is readily available to you and me; we just need to receive it. Sometimes as life happens, freedom can seem so far out of our reach. We can feel lost as we try to navigate through the different pieces of healing and deliverance. As we seek the Lord, it can feel like we don't know what we're looking for, or even where to begin to find Him. Trust that when you seek Him, He will put you on the path that leads to Him.

I had a pretty vivid dream one night that reminded me of this truth. I wasn't a part of the dream, but I was watching everything that was happening. Not quite as if I were watching a movie, but more so like I was a bystander who the others couldn't see. I was watching a group of people who were in a wooded area. They appeared to be camping. Some were sitting down while others were walking around, but it was obvious that they were all concerned and slightly panicked about something. Although I wasn't a part of their reality, I knew they were looking for someone, but they didn't know where to find him. As everyone looked around, there was a girl who said, "I don't know where he could be."

The young woman started walking towards the woods to find the man they were looking for while everyone else remained at the campsite. As she approached the woods alone, I could tell she didn't have a plan in mind and she didn't know where she was going. She was scared, but she went anyways. I saw her brightly colored bubble vest and curly hair drift off into the distance as she walked deeper into the woods.

As I was dreaming, it seemed like time blinked before my eyes. It was evident that hours had passed, even though I didn't recall time going by. Shortly after this, I saw the girl and a man approaching the campsite from the woods. Once they were closer, I could see that they both had smiles on their faces. She approached the others with excitement that she had found the man who they thought was lost. She even laughed as she told them that when she found him, he smiled and told her that he was never lost, but he was glad that she made her way through to look for him. A few seconds later, another woman appeared next to the man. I could see that her left hand was missing but the area around her wrist was glowing brightly. The man wrapped his arm around her and smiled as she looked at her wrist. As I watched them, I could see her hand starting to grow back but it was a very slow process. I didn't understand, but I could tell from her expression that she did.

I woke up at 6:47 a.m. and the Holy Spirit began interpreting the dream piece by piece. It was revealed that the man represented Jesus and the woods weren't the wilderness, but it represented freedom. Sometimes as we're walking into freedom, it can be scary, especially when it is territory that we have never stepped into before. There may be times where we don't know where to start and we may feel like we're nowhere close to finding what we're looking for. We may even have to leave behind the people who we came with to get to where Jesus is. Know that even if you have to go by yourself, you are not alone. He will direct your paths and lead you to freedom in Him.

The image of the woman's hand came back to my remembrance. The Lord showed me that although her hand was missing, it was starting to become whole again. The reason her hand was slow to grow back was to symbolize that it takes some people a little longer to be open to the healing process of their freedom. Old wounds may take longer for us to process through, but He will still be there to work through it with us. He doesn't look at us as a lost cause who is not worth healing. He desires to walk with us through the repairing and restoration stages just as He does when we become whole in Him.

In your pursuit of freedom, healing, and deliverance, it's likely that there are many things that have been cut off in your life. You've probably had to detach from people who were near and dear to your heart at one point. You've likely found yourself having to make sacrifices that have rocked you to your core. You may even feel like you've lost more than you're expected to gain and you question, "Is it worth it?" You wonder if you're even going in the right direction because you feel so far from God as you're being stripped and pruned.

Let me encourage you with the confirmation that you are right where you need to be. Jesus is proud of you for seeking Him, even when you feel like you don't even know what you're looking for. The beauty of seeking Him is the reminder that He isn't lost. He isn't hiding from you. The path that you are on may not make sense. You may not understand why you have to do it alone, but trust that it's exactly where you're supposed to be. You're right on the path that is leading you back to the heart of Christ.

There you will find joy, peace, healing, deliverance, and victory.

There you will find freedom.

The price for your freedom was bought over 2,000 years ago when Jesus' blood was shed on Calvary and when God raised Him from the dead three days later. As Jesus was nailed to the cross, He uttered the words, "It is finished," right before He died (John 19:30). He had fulfilled the assignment that His Father had sent Him to earth for. Jesus claimed the victory for all who believed in Him. When He said, "It is finished," God's plan to save mankind was solidified. The devil was defeated and sin no longer had the power to keep us bound.

Do you believe that it is finished? Do you believe that you don't have to remain the same because of what Jesus did on the cross? No longer will you remain bound. No longer will strongholds have a hold on your life. No longer will generational curses remain in your household. No longer will you walk in defeat. Your victory is finished through Christ Jesus. Your wholeness is finished through Christ Jesus. Your freedom is finished through Christ Jesus. It is finished.

So, be healed.

Be whole.

Be free, friend.

Be free.

Love you dearly,

Angel Walston

PS Stay classy, Keep it holy

Declaration:

-»»)))))————————(((((((-

Condition: say it like you believe it.

I am free. I am whole. I am an overcomer.
God chose me. God is for me. God is with me.
I am strong. I am confident. I am secure.
I am who He says I am.
I am loved. I am called. I am redeemed.
No more bondage in my life. I will not be defeated.
I am not my mistakes and I am not my past.
I am free. I am whole. I am His.

Notes:

Chapter 4:
1. "Fear." Def. 1, *Dictionary.com.* Web. 23 Sept. 2017.

Chapter 9:
1. Tarbox, P. 10 indicators a spirit of rejection is tormenting you. Above and Beyond Christian Counseling. Retrieved from https://aandbcounseling.com/10-indicators-spirit-of-rejection-tormenting/

About the Author:

Angel Walston is a woman who believed she could, and with Christ she did. She is passionate about seeing people surrendered, delivered, and made whole through Jesus Christ. In 2013, the Lord placed it on her heart to start a blog and YouTube channel to empower and equip people to know Christ and live wholeheartedly for Him. This eventually birthed her ministry, Changed Hearts, which was founded in November 2013. Since this time, God has allowed her to host conferences, speak at various women's events, and develop a passion for writing. In March 2017, she released her debut book, *Changed Heart*, which is her testimony of finding hope and redemption in Christ. She is also the author of the seven-day devotion, *Faithin' It*.

To family and friends, Angel is a tiny woman with big hair and an even bigger heart for Jesus. She loves laughing at the corniest of jokes, binge watching Netflix, and deciphering if the black spot on her bathroom floor is a spider or a ball of her thick curly hair that has shed. Her daily prayer is that she will always remain humble in the Lord's sight and that Chick-Fil-A will one day be open on Sundays.

Connect with Angel!
Changed Hearts: www.changedheartsunited.com
Store: www.changedheartsstore.com
Email: changedheartsquestions@gmail.com
YouTube: www.youtube.com/angelwalston
Instagram: angel_cheron
Facebook: Angel Walston

www.ingramcontent.com/pod-product-compliance
Lightning Source LLC
Chambersburg PA
CBHW060834110426
R18122100001BA/R181221PG42736CBX00022BA/17